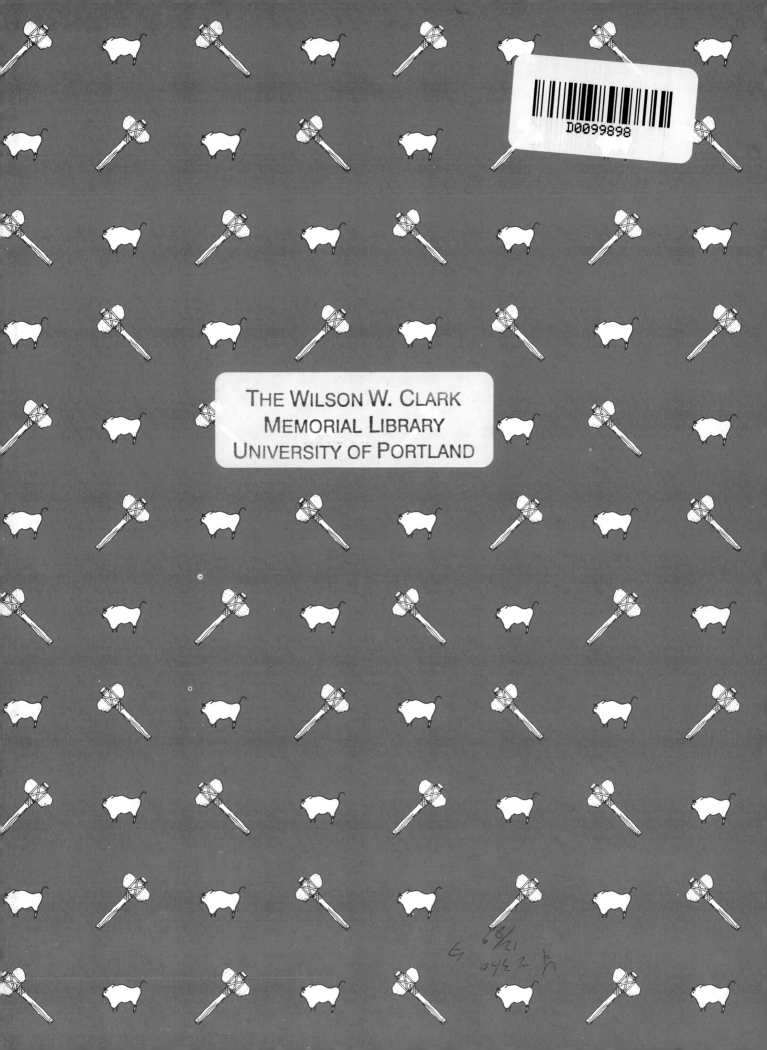

EARLY
PEOPLE

Flint Dagger,
Stone Age,
c 2,000 BC

Flint stike-a-light and
iron pyrites, Stone
Age

Coins, Iron Age,
c 50 BC - AD 50

Digging stick
(Stone-Age weight
with modern shaft)

Pottery beaker, c 2,200 BC

Terret ring, Iron
Age, c 150 BC -
AD 50

Sword, late Bronze
Age, c 950 BC

Pottery sherd, c 4,000 BC

Peruvian
mummified hand

Sage

EYEWITNESS 👁 GUIDES

Almonds

EARLY PEOPLE

Comb, Amazon rain forest

Flint handaxe, Stone Age,
c 200,000 BC

Fire and fire stones

Arrows, as
used c 6,000 BC

DORLING KINDERSLEY • LONDON

Antler harpoon point

Antler comb for preparing animal hides

This Eyewitness   Guide has been conceived by
Dorling Kindersley Limited and Editions Gallimard

Project editor Phil Wilkinson
Art editor Miranda Kennedy
Managing editor Vicky Davenport
Managing art editor Jane Owen
Special photography Dave King
Editorial Consultant Nick Merriman

First published in Great Britain in 1989
by Dorling Kindersley Limited
9 Henrietta Street, London WC2E 8PS

This edition reprinted in 1989

Copyright © 1989 Dorling Kindersley Limited, London

Soay sheep's wool
on spindle

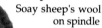

Flint arrowheads,
c 2,000 BC

British Library Cataloguing in Publication Data
Early People. - (Eyewitness)
1. Prehistoric man
I. Title   II. Series
930.1

ISBN 0-86318-342-5

Iron-Age bronze
bracelet, c 50 BC

Plumed comb,
Papua New Guinea

Colour reproduction by Colourscan, Singapore
Typeset by Windsorgraphics, Ringwood, Hampshire
Printed in Italy by A. Mondadori Editore, Verona

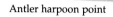

Contents

Iron-Age pin for fastening
clothes, 800-700 BC

Man or ape?

In Africa around ten million years ago, the climate was slowly changing and grassland was replacing dense forest cover. To make use of this new environment, the early apes started to spend more time on the ground. They foraged for plants and scavenged the remains of animals, and this encouraged cooperation, communication, and increased intelligence. Some of them also learned to stand upright, enabling them to look over tall grass, and leaving their hands free for other tasks. Gradually, over a period of several million years, the human tribe, known as the *Hominini*, evolved in this way. Members of the *Hominini* are distinguished from their more ape-like ancestors by their bigger brains, upright walking, and different teeth. The first groups to exhibit these features are called australopithecines ("southern apes"), and were present from four to one million years ago.

The smallest species of australopithecine, shown here with a modern woman, was the size of an upright chimpanzee. Other species were as tall as us.

OUT OF AFRICA
Australopithecines have been found only in E. and S. Africa. It is not clear whether humans first evolved in the area, or whether the fossils are just best preserved there.

EARLY BIRD
The lesser flamingo frequented shallow lakes in East Africa at the time of the earliest hominines.

ARMS AND HANDS
Lucy walked upright, so her hands were freer than those of apes. She did not make tools, but probably used convenient stones for some tasks.

IN THE GRASSLANDS
This is a reconstruction of a scene at Laetoli in East Africa about 3.75 million years ago. The region was covered by tropical grassland with lakes and a few shady trees. Early hominines foraged for food and walked upright so that they could see over the tall grass.

FOOTPRINTS IN THE ASH
In 1976, the footprints of two australo-pithecines, an adult and a child walking side by side, were found on this site. They had walked over freshly-laid volcanic ash which had then hardened.

"LUCY"
In 1974, the oldest and most complete australopithecine skeleton so far found was excavated in Ethiopia. It was named "Lucy", after the Beatles' song "Lucy in the sky with diamonds", which was playing in the excavators' camp at the time.

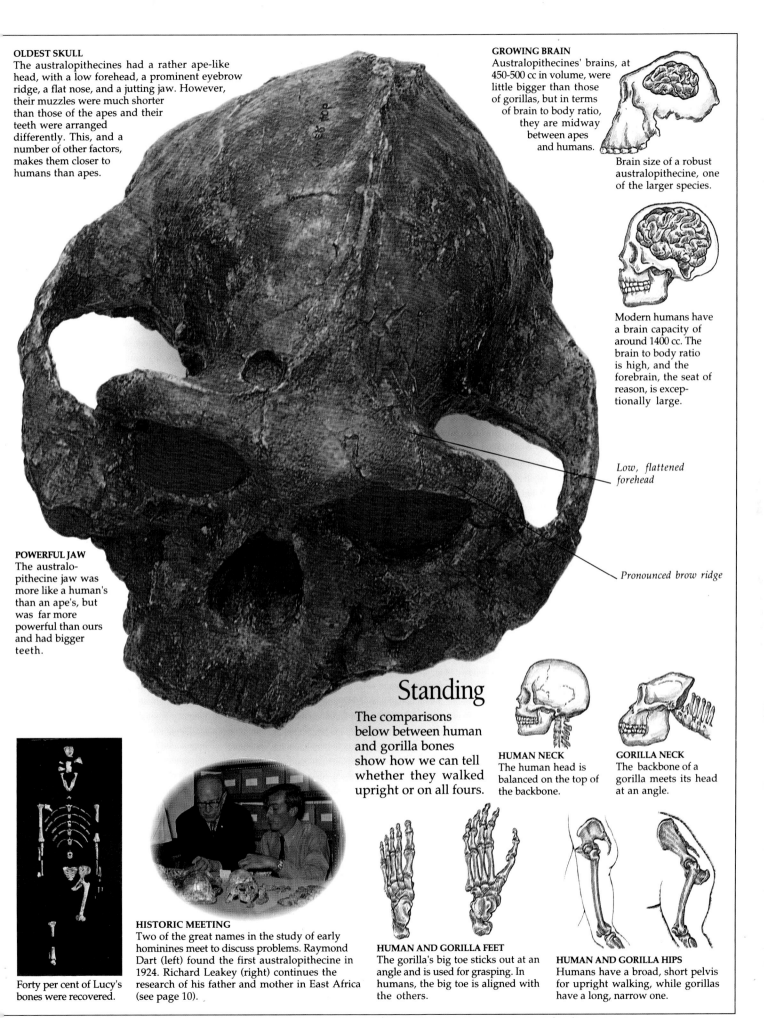

OLDEST SKULL
The australopithecines had a rather ape-like head, with a low forehead, a prominent eyebrow ridge, a flat nose, and a jutting jaw. However, their muzzles were much shorter than those of the apes and their teeth were arranged differently. This, and a number of other factors, makes them closer to humans than apes.

GROWING BRAIN
Australopithecines' brains, at 450-500 cc in volume, were little bigger than those of gorillas, but in terms of brain to body ratio, they are midway between apes and humans.

Brain size of a robust australopithecine, one of the larger species.

Modern humans have a brain capacity of around 1400 cc. The brain to body ratio is high, and the forebrain, the seat of reason, is exceptionally large.

Low, flattened forehead

Pronounced brow ridge

POWERFUL JAW
The australopithecine jaw was more like a human's than an ape's, but was far more powerful than ours and had bigger teeth.

Standing

The comparisons below between human and gorilla bones show how we can tell whether they walked upright or on all fours.

HUMAN NECK
The human head is balanced on the top of the backbone.

GORILLA NECK
The backbone of a gorilla meets its head at an angle.

Forty per cent of Lucy's bones were recovered.

HISTORIC MEETING
Two of the great names in the study of early hominines meet to discuss problems. Raymond Dart (left) found the first australopithecine in 1924. Richard Leakey (right) continues the research of his father and mother in East Africa (see page 10).

HUMAN AND GORILLA FEET
The gorilla's big toe sticks out at an angle and is used for grasping. In humans, the big toe is aligned with the others.

HUMAN AND GORILLA HIPS
Humans have a broad, short pelvis for upright walking, while gorillas have a long, narrow one.

Prehistoric food

ALTHOUGH WE DO NOT KNOW exactly what the earliest people ate, prehistoric people clearly had a very close relationship with the animals and plants around them. Through thousands of years of experience they came to know which animals to hunt, which plants they could eat, and which ones could be used to treat illnesses. Much of this knowledge has now been lost. The prehistoric diet was much more varied than our modern diet. It even included many plants that we think of as weeds. After people started to grow corn (see pages 30-31), nutritious wild foods were still eaten. These foods could only be preserved by drying, salting, or pickling, so the seasons had a strong effect on what was eaten. Another difference from our diet was that there were few sweeteners, except for honey.

NETTLES
The young leaves of nettles were made into a soup. Nettle juice can help in cheese making.

Rue

Catmint

MEDICINE
As well as being nutritious, many plants have medicinal properties that have been exploited for thousands of years. The leaves of rue were used for headaches; catmint was an ancient cold cure.

Wheat grains

An imaginative reconstruction of Stone-Age hunter-gatherers preparing and cooking food.

Dandelion leaves

Sunflower seeds

SALAD DAYS
Although now thought of as a weed, dandelion leaves were a regular salad food in prehistoric times.

Hazelnuts

Juniper berries

Hazel twig

Almonds

FROM THE WOODS
Woodlands yielded an abundant supply of wild nuts and berries, which are excellent sources of food. They are also useful because they can easily be stored. Hazelnuts in particular seem to have been stored for the winter, and fruit could be preserved in the form of jam. In the Near East, wheat grains were first collected wild, and then cultivated. Juniper berries made a savoury spice.

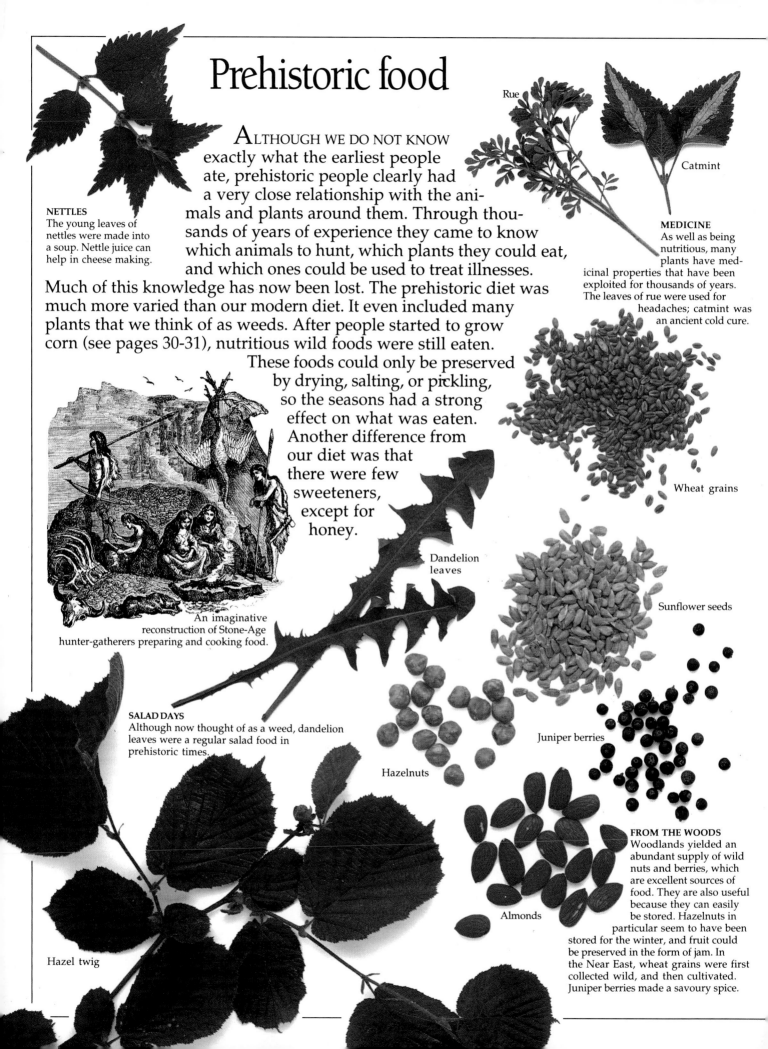

FOODS FOR THE FAMILY
As far as we know from recent societies, prehistoric hunter-gatherers benefitted from a very broad diet, and each member of the family played their part in providing food. The men hunted wild animals, such as the stag shown here. The bulk of the food, however, was often gathered by the women and children. This consisted of such items as plants, eggs, nuts, and perhaps fish.

Quails' eggs

FRUIT
Fruit was an important food for early Mediterranean peoples. As well as being a rich source of nutrition, it could be dried and stored. Grapes could also be made into wine.

Figs

Dates

SALMON
From at least 10,000 BC, people used large spears to catch salmon in the rivers of Europe.

Fenugreek

SPICE OF LIFE
Besides salt, which was used more to preserve food than to flavour it, a variety of seasonings and spices have a long history. Some, such as coriander, were also prized because they stimulated the digestive system.

Coriander

Black cumin

Mustard

Peppercorns

Seals were good food sources for northern peoples.

HUNTING
This cave painting shows men hunting giant elk.

Basil

Mint

Sage

COOKING MEAT
This is a reconstruction of one ancient method of cooking meat. The joint was wrapped in a leather parcel and secured with a twig. This was put into a pot of water brought to boiling point by dropping in red hot stones which had been heated in a fire (see pages 16-17). The more usual method of cooking meat was by grilling or roasting it over the glowing embers of a fire using a spit. Roasting could also be done using a heated stone-lined pit.

HERBS
In prehistoric times, as now, herbs were often gathered to flavour food.

The toolmakers

ABOUT TWO MILLION YEARS AGO one of the australopithecine species evolved into the other member of the human tribe, the genus *Homo*. Compared with australopithecus, *Homo* had a bigger brain, a more human-looking face, and hip bones that were better adapted both to walking upright and to giving birth to babies with large heads. The earliest species of the genus *Homo* could make tools and was therefore named *Homo habilis* ("handy man"). Toolmaking involves using memory, planning ahead, and working out abstract problems; it marks the beginning of our use of culture to help us to adapt to our surroundings - a uniquely human ability. The habilines probably also used some primitive form of communication to pass on knowledge. They seem to have used their tools to cut meat and smash open bones for marrow. They may possibly have hunted animals, but it is more likely that they scavenged abandoned carcases, and that plants were still their major source of food. There is evidence that they also made small, round huts to shelter in - the earliest buildings in the world. They lived in East Africa, and related groups may have lived in South Africa and Southeast Asia.

PEBBLE TOOL
There is a great difference between using tools and manufacturing them. Chimpanzees may select certain items and even modify them for use as tools, but humans are the only animals to use one set of tools to make other tools. This pebble tool comes from Olduvai Gorge in Tanzania.

The Piltdown forgery

Earlier this century, scientists were looking for a "missing link" between humans and apes. Between 1912 and 1915 amateur archaeologist Charles Dawson, and later Sir Arthur Smith Woodward of the British Museum, found a human skull with an ape's jaw in a gravel pit at Piltdown, Sussex, together with the bones of extinct animals. For years "Piltdown man" was accepted until in 1953 it was shown to be an elaborate forgery. Who carried out the hoax is still uncertain.

Sir Arthur Smith Woodward of the British Museum.

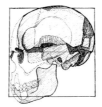

This is how it was thought the fragments of the skull fitted together.

Orang-utan skull

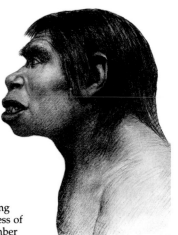

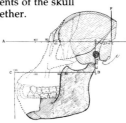

This old drawing of an Orang-utan emphasizes its human-like characteristics.

PILTDOWN RECONSTRUCTION
So eager were scientists to find a missing link that many accepted the genuineness of Piltdown man immediately, and a number of reconstructions such as this one were soon made.

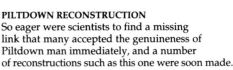

THE LEAKEY FAMILY
The Leakey family have been involved in research in East Africa for nearly sixty years. In 1960, years of patient work paid off for Louis Leakey and his wife Mary when they found and named the first *Homo habilis*. Their son, Richard, pictured here, has continued their work in Ethiopia, finding many more hominine remains.

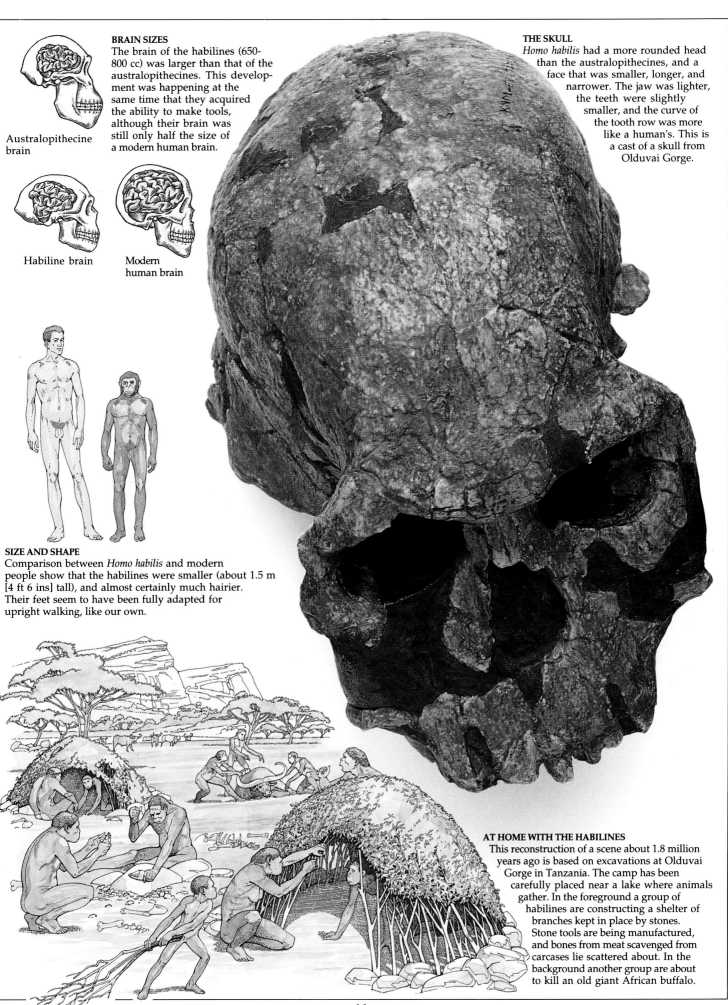

BRAIN SIZES
The brain of the habilines (650-800 cc) was larger than that of the australopithecines. This development was happening at the same time that they acquired the ability to make tools, although their brain was still only half the size of a modern human brain.

Australopithecine brain

Habiline brain

Modern human brain

THE SKULL
Homo habilis had a more rounded head than the australopithecines, and a face that was smaller, longer, and narrower. The jaw was lighter, the teeth were slightly smaller, and the curve of the tooth row was more like a human's. This is a cast of a skull from Olduvai Gorge.

SIZE AND SHAPE
Comparison between *Homo habilis* and modern people show that the habilines were smaller (about 1.5 m [4 ft 6 ins] tall), and almost certainly much hairier. Their feet seem to have been fully adapted for upright walking, like our own.

AT HOME WITH THE HABILINES
This reconstruction of a scene about 1.8 million years ago is based on excavations at Olduvai Gorge in Tanzania. The camp has been carefully placed near a lake where animals gather. In the foreground a group of habilines are constructing a shelter of branches kept in place by stones. Stone tools are being manufactured, and bones from meat scavenged from carcases lie scattered about. In the background another group are about to kill an old giant African buffalo.

Flintworking

THE FIRST TOOL-MAKING HUMAN, *Homo habilis*, made simple pebble-tools from various types of rock (see pages 10-11). Later, in Europe, people found that flint was the most suitable material, and flint tools half a million years old have been found. Flint's most useful property is that regular flakes come off when it is chipped. The angle and size of the flakes can be controlled by careful chipping, and so a variety of sizes and shapes can be made. Because it is rather like glass, flint takes a very sharp edge which can be resharpened by further flaking when it is blunt. Flint is widespread and abundant, though in many cases it has to be mined from the chalk in which it occurs. The earliest tools were made by removing flakes from a core of flint until the required shape was left. Most handaxes were made in this way. Later on, the flakes themselves were used to make finer tools and weapons, like knives and arrowheads.

FIRST IN BRITAIN
This handaxe is about a quarter of a million years old. It comes from Swanscombe, one of the oldest sites in Britain, where the earliest British human skull has been found.

Rounded end used as hammer head

Flat striking platform

CORE
In the earliest tools the core itself formed the tool. Later the flakes were used.

HAMMERSTONE
A pebble hammer like this was the simplest tool used for flintworking. The unworked flint was struck with the hammer, and large, thick flakes came away.

Flint flake

Flint flake

2 REMOVING FLAKES
A stone hammer was used to strike a sharp blow along the edge of the rough-cut flint. This detached a large chip from the underside.

ANTLER HAMMER
A light bone or antler hammer was used for detaching smaller, thinner chips of flint.

1 SHAPING THE CORE
The first step in flintworking was to select a piece of flint and to start trimming it to a rough shape.

3 FINISHING
The axe was trimmed by striking it along its edge with a bone hammer.

FLINT FLAKES
Long, thin blades such as these are made by preparing a flat platform on a core and striking the outside rim vertically with a bone hammer.

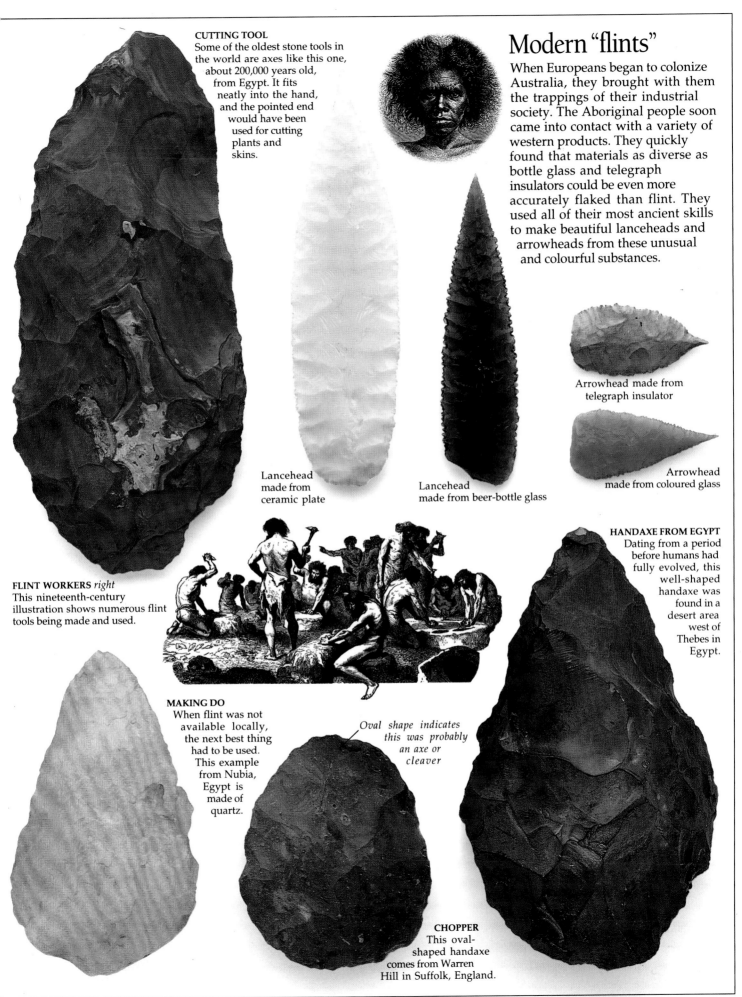

CUTTING TOOL
Some of the oldest stone tools in the world are axes like this one, about 200,000 years old, from Egypt. It fits neatly into the hand, and the pointed end would have been used for cutting plants and skins.

Modern "flints"

When Europeans began to colonize Australia, they brought with them the trappings of their industrial society. The Aboriginal people soon came into contact with a variety of western products. They quickly found that materials as diverse as bottle glass and telegraph insulators could be even more accurately flaked than flint. They used all of their most ancient skills to make beautiful lanceheads and arrowheads from these unusual and colourful substances.

Arrowhead made from telegraph insulator

Arrowhead made from coloured glass

Lancehead made from ceramic plate

Lancehead made from beer-bottle glass

HANDAXE FROM EGYPT
Dating from a period before humans had fully evolved, this well-shaped handaxe was found in a desert area west of Thebes in Egypt.

FLINT WORKERS *right*
This nineteenth-century illustration shows numerous flint tools being made and used.

MAKING DO
When flint was not available locally, the next best thing had to be used. This example from Nubia, Egypt is made of quartz.

Oval shape indicates this was probably an axe or cleaver

CHOPPER
This oval-shaped handaxe comes from Warren Hill in Suffolk, England.

Moving northwards

BETWEEN ABOUT 1.6 million and 200,000 years ago lived the *Homo erectus* people. They had bigger brains and bodies than the habilines, and some were probably as tall and as heavy as ourselves. They were also much more advanced than the habilines - they had a more varied toolkit and knew how to use fire. Fire provided a focus for the family group, kept people warm, and could be used for cooking. In addition it kept predators away and helped in hunting - animals could be driven into traps using fire. These skills, and the increased brain power that goes with them, enabled these people to exploit a much wider range of environments than their ancestors. They were probably the first people to range beyond Africa into Europe and Asia, where most of their fossils have in fact been found. In these new environments, the harshest of which would have been Ice-Age Europe, *Homo erectus* gradually adapted to local conditions. Over a million years, they evolved differently in different parts of the world, but the fossils still share enough general characteristics to show they are clear ancestors of ours.

THE SPREAD OF *HOMO ERECTUS*
Although *Homo erectus* probably started life in Africa, remains have been found in places as far away as China and Java. They colonized these areas by making short outward migrations into new territory away from each generation's family base.

WOOLLY RHINOCEROS
Homo erectus survived until well into the Ice Age, when, in Europe, colder conditions came and went at intervals of several thousand years (see pages 18-19). The woolly rhinoceros was one of the large mammals adapted to this climate which *erectus* may have hunted.

Stick held in hand _____

FIRE STICKS
The earliest hominines might have made occasional use of natural fires caused by lightning, but *Homo erectus* seems to have been the first to create fire deliberately and to use it systematically. A simple wooden tool like this would have been used to make fire.

Groove to take stick _____

_____ Wooden hearth

FIRE-MAKERS
This scene shows a band of *Homo erectus* people in front of the cave they are using for shelter. On the right a male is starting to make a handaxe by removing flakes from a flint core with a hammerstone (see page 12). The female next to him is kindling a fire in a hearth surrounded by a stones to shelter it from the wind. The people in the background are using handaxes to butcher a large mammal they have hunted. The joints will then be cooked over the open fire.

A MORE HUMAN HEAD
The skull of *Homo erectus* has several features that make it look more human than that of the habilines. The brain is larger, ranging from 880 to 1100 cc in volume (compared with an average of 1400 cc for modern humans). The teeth are smaller than those of *Homo habilis*. But the skull of Homo erectus is still different from a modern skull in many ways. It is very thick, with a sloping forehead and a large eyebrow ridge; there is a relatively massive jaw, flat face, and no chin; and the large jaw and teeth needed strong muscles to keep the head upright - these were attached to a bony bump at the back of the head.

Slight crest in the centre of the skull for the attachment of powerful muscles

Long, low skull

Shelving forehead

Strong eyebrow ridge

Lower jaw (not shown) joins skull here

Teeth smaller than those of Homo habilis, *but bigger than modern man's*

A NEW TYPE OF TOOL
The handaxe was the distinctive new type of tool produced by *Homo erectus*. The broad end was held in the fist, and the axe was used for cutting meat or digging up edible roots. Handaxes spread over the Old World and remained in use for about one-and-a-half million years.

EVIDENCE FOR FIRE *above and right*
Some of the earliest evidence for human use of fire comes from a cave at Choukoutien near Beijing, China. Inside, a large number of *Homo erectus* remains were found, dating back to 360,000 years ago. A deep layer of ash showed prolonged use of fire, as did large lumps of charcoal (right) and burnt bone from animals that had been killed and eaten (above).

15

The coming of fire

FIRE WAS ONE OF THE MOST IMPORTANT DISCOVERIES ever made by ancient people. It not only enabled them to keep warm when the temperature was very much colder than it is today, it was also useful in keeping wild animals away, in roasting meat, and in hardening the tips of wooden spears. Before they learned to make fire, people probably used accidental fires caused by lightning. The great step forward was made when they found out how to make fire for themselves by rubbing two sticks together to create a spark. The earliest evidence we have of fire is from about a quarter of a million years ago. Because no fire-making equipment survives from this remote period, archaeologists have to rely upon studies of more recent societies around the world who probably made fire as their brothers and sisters did long, long ago.

FIRE IN THE ICE AGE
This is a reconstruction of fire-making in a cave during one of the Ice Ages about 200,000 years ago. A simple fire drill is being rotated at speed over a piece of dry timber.

Wooden mouthpiece

Wooden drill

Wooden drill

Leather bow

Dry straw

Wooden hearth

Holes where drill has been used

BOW DRILL
On this modern model of a bow drill, the leather bow makes it easy to turn the drill fast and generate enough heat to start a fire.

Using a bow drill

Wooden hearth

FIRE DRILL
This simple fire drill from Akamba, Kenya shows the basic principle of generating heat by turning the drill so the wood underneath begins to smoulder and burn.

Rotating the drill

AROUND THE HEARTH
In the sort of fire produced by the earliest fire-makers, the tinder ignited by the fire drill was added to a heap of dry grass and small sticks. Larger pieces were added once the fire was alight. A circle of large stones helped to protect it from draughts.

TWO DRY STICKS
In the Stone Age, before the fire drill had been perfected, fire could still be made by rubbing together two dry sticks. Brushwood was used to keep the fire going.

Sticks would be built up as the fire started to burn

As the stones got hot they could be used to heat water for cooking

AFRICAN FIRE-MAKING
Some peoples in Africa used the simple wooden drill to make fire until the beginning of this century. Much of our knowledge of early fire-making techniques comes from studies of these people.

Life in the Ice Age

THE "ICE AGE" consisted of several alternate cold and warm periods, each lasting tens of thousands of years. During some of these periods the climate was actually warmer than it is today, and only for parts of the period was there extensive ice coverage of northern Europe. The *Homo erectus* people were the first to live in this area, probably only in the warm periods. By 250,000 years ago, people were slowly adapting to living in the cold periods, and 150,000 years later the first distinct subspecies of modern humans, *Homo sapiens neanderthalensis*, can be recognized. Neanderthals were very similar to people today, and if they were dressed in modern clothes, they would not attract any attention. They would just be slightly smaller, stockier, and heavier-featured than average. Those found in the warmer Mediterranean areas were even more modern-looking. Neanderthals show the first stirrings of humanness: they cared for the disabled, buried their dead carefully, and probably had some sort of religion. They were abruptly replaced about 35,000 years ago by fully modern people, *Homo sapiens sapiens*, who had been evolving in the meantime in the warmer climate of Africa. They colonized huge areas of the world at this time, including Europe in its final icy phase, and even Australia.

THE ICE AGE AND THE NEANDERTHALS
This map shows the maximum extent of the ice sheets (blue), and the land exposed by the consequent lowering of the sea level. The spread of Neanderthals over a period of 60,000 years is indicated in brown, and the red dot shows the Neander Valley in Germany, where the first find was made in 1856.

HOME ON THE TUNDRA
When *Homo sapiens sapiens* colonized the cold Russian tundra, they used methods of house-building employed by the Neanderthals. This reconstruction shows a dwelling excavated at Pushkari, consisting of sewn skins stretched over a frame of poles, weighted down by mammoth bones.

MAMMOTH-BONE HUTS
Remarkable evidence of Neanderthal huts has been found in the Russian Ukraine. They were made of animal skins on a frame of branches or mammoth long bones, and the outsides were heavily weighted with more bones.

THE NEANDERTHAL WARDROBE
Neanderthals were probably the first humans to wear clothes all the time, to protect themselves from the cold. When making clothes, they would begin by stretching out an animal hide such as a deerskin, and use flint tools to scrape it clean of fat and sinews. After tanning, they would sew the hide into the required shape.

TOOLMAKING
Neanderthal toolkits are a great improvement on those used by *Homo erectus*. They could produce a wide range of fine tools for a variety of tasks. Bone and antler were extensively used, as well as flint.

LIFE IN A COLD CLIMATE
Neanderthals were well adapted for living in a cold climate, and their lifestyle may have resembled that of some of the Inuit people (see pages 20-21). They probably lived in extended family groups, each member of which would carry out a variety of tasks. This scene reflects the diversity of this first truly human group.

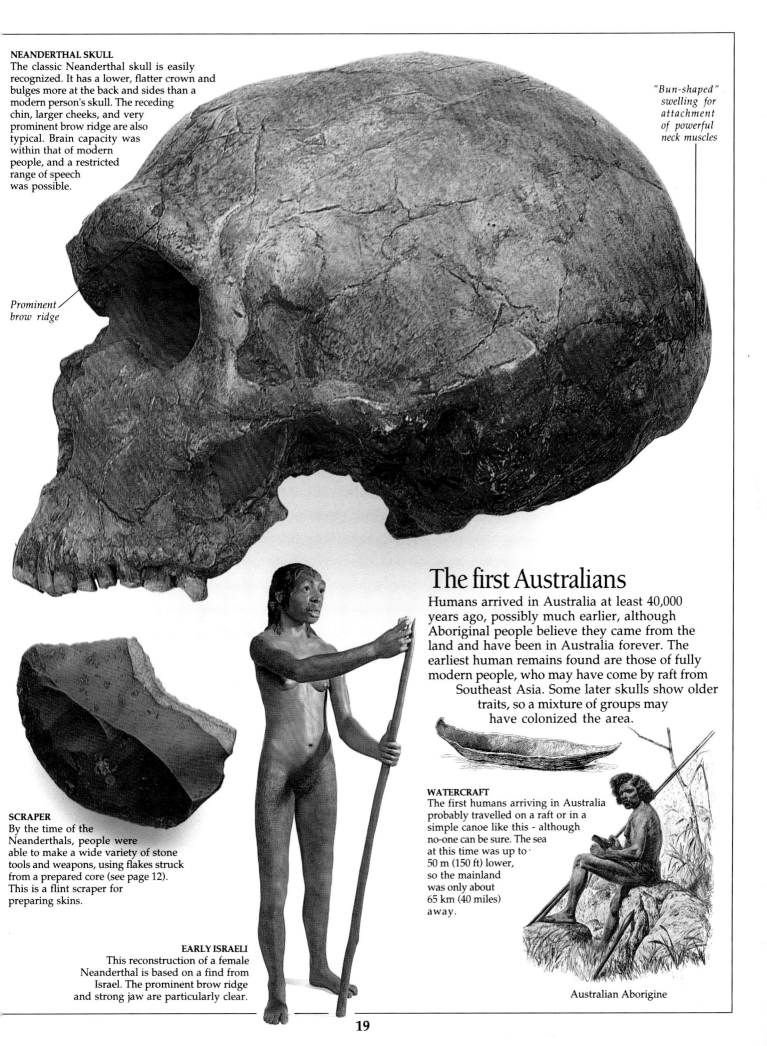

NEANDERTHAL SKULL
The classic Neanderthal skull is easily recognized. It has a lower, flatter crown and bulges more at the back and sides than a modern person's skull. The receding chin, larger cheeks, and very prominent brow ridge are also typical. Brain capacity was within that of modern people, and a restricted range of speech was possible.

"Bun-shaped" swelling for attachment of powerful neck muscles

Prominent brow ridge

The first Australians

Humans arrived in Australia at least 40,000 years ago, possibly much earlier, although Aboriginal people believe they came from the land and have been in Australia forever. The earliest human remains found are those of fully modern people, who may have come by raft from Southeast Asia. Some later skulls show older traits, so a mixture of groups may have colonized the area.

SCRAPER
By the time of the Neanderthals, people were able to make a wide variety of stone tools and weapons, using flakes struck from a prepared core (see page 12). This is a flint scraper for preparing skins.

WATERCRAFT
The first humans arriving in Australia probably travelled on a raft or in a simple canoe like this - although no-one can be sure. The sea at this time was up to 50 m (150 ft) lower, so the mainland was only about 65 km (40 miles) away.

EARLY ISRAELI
This reconstruction of a female Neanderthal is based on a find from Israel. The prominent brow ridge and strong jaw are particularly clear.

Australian Aborigine

Ice-Age hunters

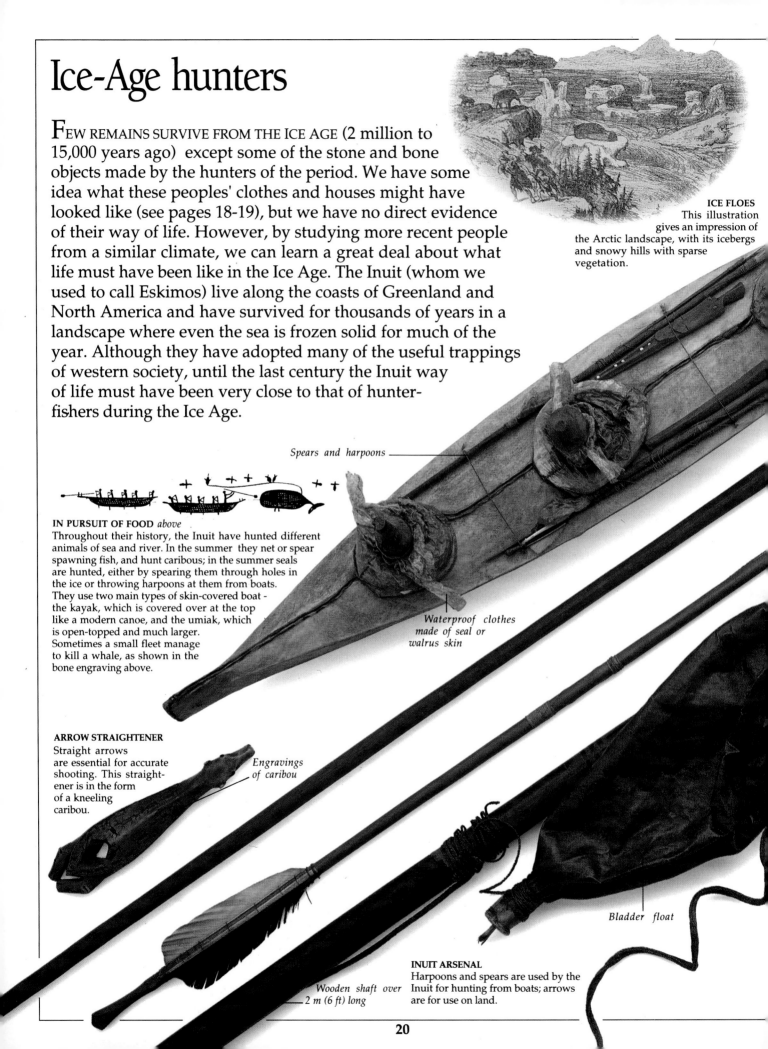

FEW REMAINS SURVIVE FROM THE ICE AGE (2 million to 15,000 years ago) except some of the stone and bone objects made by the hunters of the period. We have some idea what these peoples' clothes and houses might have looked like (see pages 18-19), but we have no direct evidence of their way of life. However, by studying more recent people from a similar climate, we can learn a great deal about what life must have been like in the Ice Age. The Inuit (whom we used to call Eskimos) live along the coasts of Greenland and North America and have survived for thousands of years in a landscape where even the sea is frozen solid for much of the year. Although they have adopted many of the useful trappings of western society, until the last century the Inuit way of life must have been very close to that of hunter-fishers during the Ice Age.

ICE FLOES
This illustration gives an impression of the Arctic landscape, with its icebergs and snowy hills with sparse vegetation.

Spears and harpoons

IN PURSUIT OF FOOD *above*
Throughout their history, the Inuit have hunted different animals of sea and river. In the summer they net or spear spawning fish, and hunt caribous; in the summer seals are hunted, either by spearing them through holes in the ice or throwing harpoons at them from boats. They use two main types of skin-covered boat - the kayak, which is covered over at the top like a modern canoe, and the umiak, which is open-topped and much larger. Sometimes a small fleet manage to kill a whale, as shown in the bone engraving above.

Waterproof clothes made of seal or walrus skin

ARROW STRAIGHTENER
Straight arrows are essential for accurate shooting. This straight-ener is in the form of a kneeling caribou.

Engravings of caribou

Bladder float

Wooden shaft over 2 m (6 ft) long

INUIT ARSENAL
Harpoons and spears are used by the Inuit for hunting from boats; arrows are for use on land.

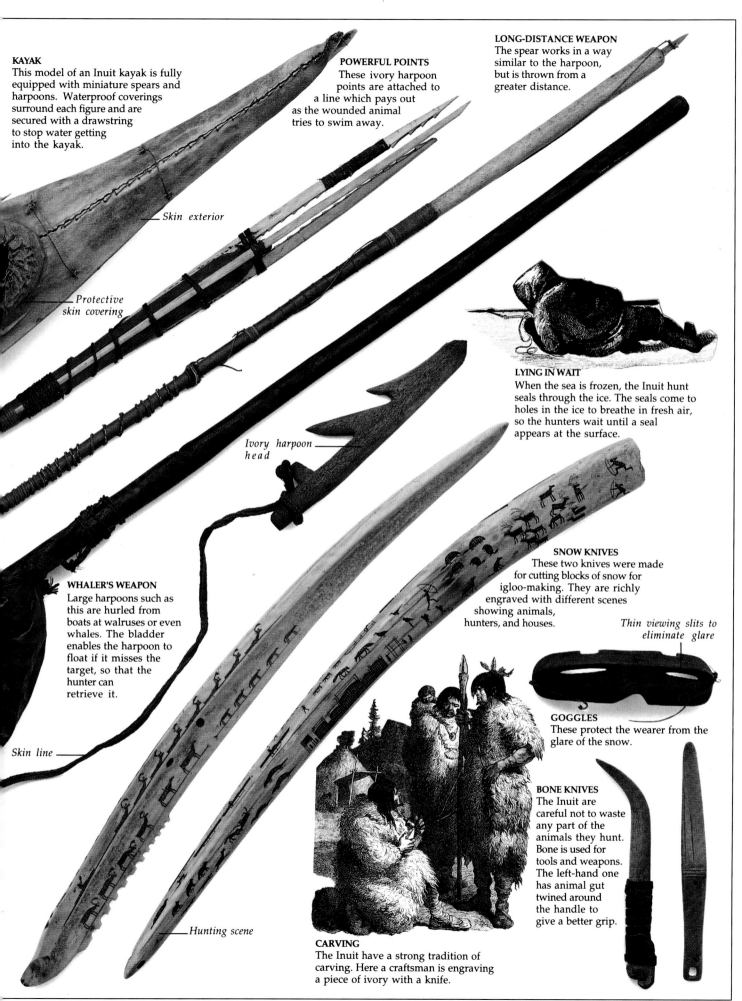

KAYAK
This model of an Inuit kayak is fully equipped with miniature spears and harpoons. Waterproof coverings surround each figure and are secured with a drawstring to stop water getting into the kayak.

Skin exterior

Protective skin covering

POWERFUL POINTS
These ivory harpoon points are attached to a line which pays out as the wounded animal tries to swim away.

LONG-DISTANCE WEAPON
The spear works in a way similar to the harpoon, but is thrown from a greater distance.

Ivory harpoon head

LYING IN WAIT
When the sea is frozen, the Inuit hunt seals through the ice. The seals come to holes in the ice to breathe in fresh air, so the hunters wait until a seal appears at the surface.

WHALER'S WEAPON
Large harpoons such as this are hurled from boats at walruses or even whales. The bladder enables the harpoon to float if it misses the target, so that the hunter can retrieve it.

Skin line

SNOW KNIVES
These two knives were made for cutting blocks of snow for igloo-making. They are richly engraved with different scenes showing animals, hunters, and houses.

Thin viewing slits to eliminate glare

GOGGLES
These protect the wearer from the glare of the snow.

BONE KNIVES
The Inuit are careful not to waste any part of the animals they hunt. Bone is used for tools and weapons. The left-hand one has animal gut twined around the handle to give a better grip.

Hunting scene

CARVING
The Inuit have a strong tradition of carving. Here a craftsman is engraving a piece of ivory with a knife.

Modern humans

MOST EXPERTS BELIEVE that the subspecies to which we belong, *Homo sapiens sapiens*, evolved in Africa around 100,000 years ago. By 30,000 years ago, *sapiens* had spread to all parts of the world apart from the Americas, and by at least 11,000 years ago, every continent apart from Antarctica was populated. Interbreeding with local peoples might have produced the different races that inhabit the world today. *Homo sapiens sapiens* developed several skills and patterns of behaviour that were seen dimly among the Neanderthals. Communication through the spoken word and art became a vital part of human life; people carefully buried their dead and had some concept of religion and an afterlife; and hunting skills probably reached their peak. Later human developments - farming, civilization, huge population growth, industry, and control over nature, have occurred in the relatively tiny period of ten thousand years.

PAINTED HAND
About 20,000 years ago in the cave at Pech-Merle in France, someone produced this "negative" hand by placing their own hand on the wall and painting over it. The hand, the part of us that makes and uses implements and is used for signalling, is a powerful symbol.

"Venus" figurine in stone from Willendorf, Austria (cast)

Stylized female figure from Corsica, c 3,500 BC

WORKS OF ART
Although the Neanderthals were the first to show some artistic sense by scratching simple designs on bones, it was not until the arrival of *Homo sapiens sapiens* that painting and sculpture developed fully.

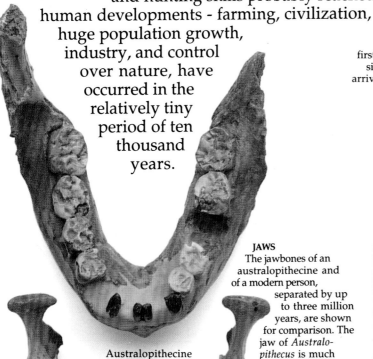

JAWS
The jawbones of an australopithecine and of a modern person, separated by up to three million years, are shown for comparison. The jaw of *Australopithecus* is much larger and has much bigger back teeth.

Australopithecine jawbone

Modern human jawbone

CARVERS
Victorian illustrators imagined that the sculptors of the end of the Ice Age looked like modern Inuit people. Although they did not carve images exactly like the ones shown here, they would certainly have dressed in furs and used deer antlers as a material.

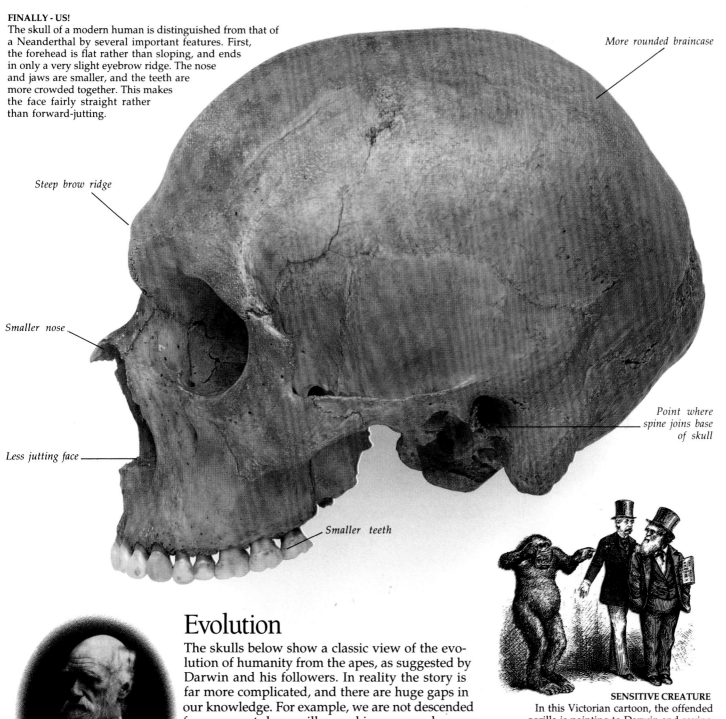

FINALLY - US!
The skull of a modern human is distinguished from that of a Neanderthal by several important features. First, the forehead is flat rather than sloping, and ends in only a very slight eyebrow ridge. The nose and jaws are smaller, and the teeth are more crowded together. This makes the face fairly straight rather than forward-jutting.

More rounded braincase

Steep brow ridge

Smaller nose

Point where spine joins base of skull

Less jutting face

Smaller teeth

Evolution

The skulls below show a classic view of the evolution of humanity from the apes, as suggested by Darwin and his followers. In reality the story is far more complicated, and there are huge gaps in our knowledge. For example, we are not descended from present-day gorillas or chimpanzees, because they have been evolving too. But apes and modern people may share some ancestors. In addition, there has not been a smooth progress, but a series of fits and starts, with many species around at the same time, some surviving, others becoming extinct.

Charles Darwin (1809-82) first publicized the idea of evolution.

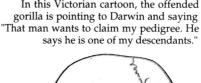

SENSITIVE CREATURE
In this Victorian cartoon, the offended gorilla is pointing to Darwin and saying "That man wants to claim my pedigree. He says he is one of my descendants."

Skull of primitive reptile (230-195 million years old)

Skull of mammal (54-16 million years old)

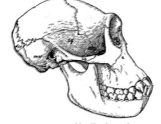

Skull of modern chimpanzee

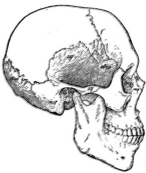

Skull of modern man

The first artists

MASTERPIECE OF CAVE ART
This painting is in a cave at Altamira, Spain.

THE EARLIEST WORKS OF ART were created around 30,000 years ago, during the last Ice Age. Because the making of art is distinctive to mankind, we can say with confidence that by this period the creators of such works were truly human. These early works of art take two main forms. The most famous are the vivid paintings of animals which cover the walls and roofs of caves, such as those at Lascaux in France and Altamira in Spain. The other, less well-known, type consists of small sculptures and relief carvings of animals and female figures. These have also been found in caves, but they occur in larger numbers in open-air sites in eastern Europe. Decoration became popular again when pottery was invented.

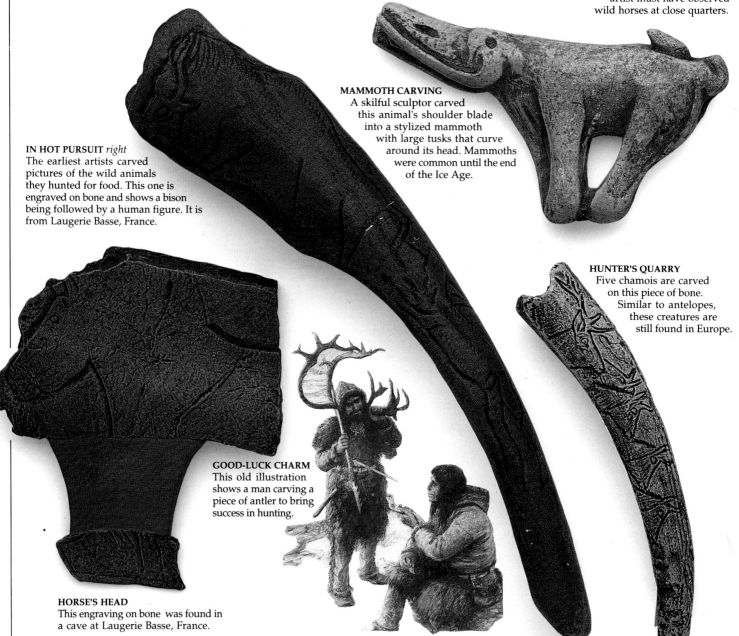

From the cave of Mas d'Azil, France

HORSES' HEADS
The accuracy of these carvings shows that the artist must have observed wild horses at close quarters.

MAMMOTH CARVING
A skilful sculptor carved this animal's shoulder blade into a stylized mammoth with large tusks that curve around its head. Mammoths were common until the end of the Ice Age.

IN HOT PURSUIT *right*
The earliest artists carved pictures of the wild animals they hunted for food. This one is engraved on bone and shows a bison being followed by a human figure. It is from Laugerie Basse, France.

HUNTER'S QUARRY
Five chamois are carved on this piece of bone. Similar to antelopes, these creatures are still found in Europe.

GOOD-LUCK CHARM
This old illustration shows a man carving a piece of antler to bring success in hunting.

HORSE'S HEAD
This engraving on bone was found in a cave at Laugerie Basse, France.

MAKING THE COLOURS *right*
In this reconstruction, an artist is grinding up a pigment to make paint. Early artists used earth colours such as ochres, and pigments made from other naturally occuring minerals.

PATTERNED PLAQUE
This plaque, made from a type of stone called schist, was produced over 4,000 years after cave painting had died out, and is engraved in a quite diferent, abstract, geometric style. It was found in a large stone tomb at Alentjo, Portugal, and dates from the New Stone Age, (c 4,000 BC).

ARTISTS AT WORK
This artist is painting the animals he is going to hunt. This activity would have formed part of his religious ritual. Light for the painters was provided by burning fat in a lamp.

Marble figurine from Melos, Greece, c 2,500-2,000 BC

PAINTED POTTERY
As well as being useful, pottery could bear striking painted and engraved decorations. This example is about 6,000 years old and comes from Rumania.

BISON
This is another painting from the famous Spanish cave at Altamira.

Found at the site of Lespugue, France

MYSTERIOUS FIGURES
These so-called "Venus figurines" have been found right across Europe from Spain to Russia, and date from c 25,000-15,000 BC. They are always faceless, and heavily pregnant. They seem to show the importance placed on reproduction and the survival of the species.

From Brno, Czechoslovakia

THE POTTER'S ART
The decoration on many early pots was engraved in the surface of the clay.

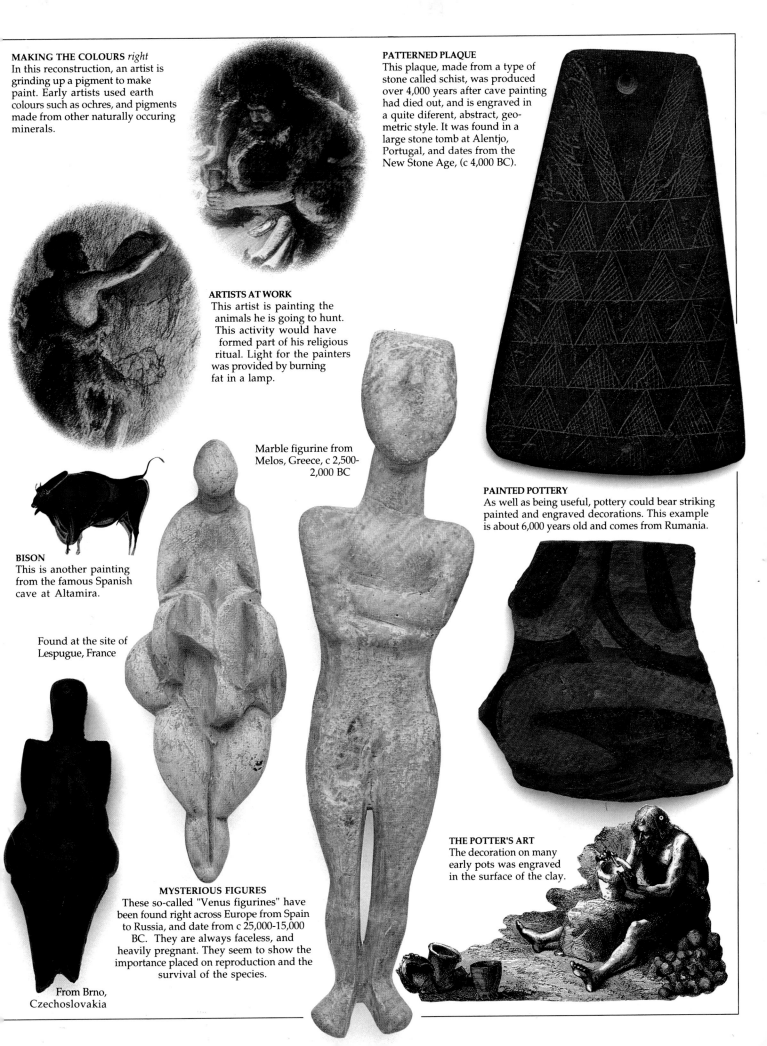

Hunting and gathering

FOR NINETY-NINE PER CENT of their time on earth, humans have survived by hunting animals and gathering plants for food. During the Ice Age, people in Europe were probably hunting big game such as the woolly mammoth. About 75,000 years ago people on the coast of South Africa were catching seals and penguins; and 25,000 years ago the first Australians were hunting now-extinct giant kangaroos. Throughout the prehistoric period, it is likely that most of the hunter-gatherers' food came from plants, nuts, fruits, and shellfish, because these could be gathered with little effort. Their remains do not survive as well as bones, however, so they are not often found on archaeological sites. But the discovery of flint spear- and arrow-heads suggests that early peoples also had evolved quite sophisticated methods of hunting game.

STONE-AGE HUNTERS
Both spears and bows and arrows were used to hunt for food in the Stone Age.

Bark "plate"

Blackberries

FRUIT AND NUTS
Remains of these high-energy foods have been found preserved in hunters' camps from 12,000 years ago.

Hazelnuts

HARPOON POINT
This point is made of antler, and is about 10,000 years old.

Antler is easily made into harpoons like these

FISHING TACKLE *above*
Found near London, this harpoon would have been used for spearing fish from a sandbank at the river's edge. It dates from c 8,000 BC.

Twine binding

SIMPLE BUT DEADLY *above and below*
Two halves of a reproduction middle Stone Age arrow. The bow and arrow were developed to hunt the shy forest animals from a distance.

Flight of duck feathers

Fire-hardened wooden point

Reproduction wooden shaft

FLINT ARROW
Arrows like this were used about 8,000 years ago. The head was stuck in place with birch resin glue.

Flints glued in groove cut in shaft

Reproduction shaft

Antler sleeve

Alternative method of binding

DIGGER
In their search
for wild food,
early hunters
and gatherers
would weight
a stick and use
it to dig up
edible roots
and grubs.

Wedge to prevent movement

DUAL-PURPOSE TOOL
This adze head is fitted into an antler sleeve and secured
to the handle by a leather thong. It may have been used for
digging up edible roots or for woodworking.

Wooden sleeve

Head dates from c 10,000-4,000 BC

Perforated quartzite pebble

FINEST FLINTS
In the early
Bronze Age, a
variety of finely
worked flint
arrowheads were
produced. Some
were shaped
ornately.

SMALL FLINT ADZE
An adze has an
asymmetrical cutting edge
and is mounted with the
blade at right-angles to the
handle. Used to cut wood, it
is usually swung down, often
between the legs. This one is
inserted into a wooden
sleeve and secured with
animal glue or resin.

HUNTER'S PREY
Cave paintings, some 20,000
years old, often show animals
that were hunted at the time,
like this deer in the
Dordogne, France.

Iron pyrites

Reproduction wooden handles

Traditional shape

Flint strike-a-light

FIRE-MAKING
If the iron pyrites is
hit with the flint, a
spark is produced. This will
fall on dry grass and can be
fanned into a flame.

Missing shaft

Incurved design

This reindeer is being
butchered with a stone axe.

Modern wooden stick

27

Desert hunters

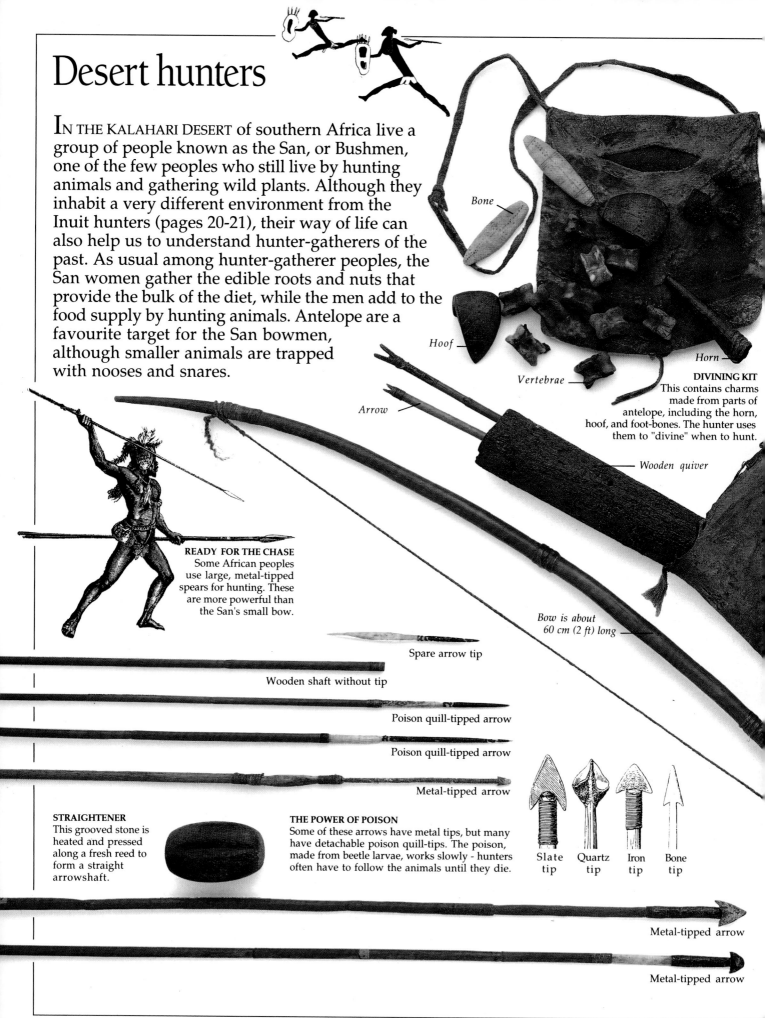

IN THE KALAHARI DESERT of southern Africa live a group of people known as the San, or Bushmen, one of the few peoples who still live by hunting animals and gathering wild plants. Although they inhabit a very different environment from the Inuit hunters (pages 20-21), their way of life can also help us to understand hunter-gatherers of the past. As usual among hunter-gatherer peoples, the San women gather the edible roots and nuts that provide the bulk of the diet, while the men add to the food supply by hunting animals. Antelope are a favourite target for the San bowmen, although smaller animals are trapped with nooses and snares.

Bone

Hoof

Vertebrae

Arrow

Horn

DIVINING KIT
This contains charms made from parts of antelope, including the horn, hoof, and foot-bones. The hunter uses them to "divine" when to hunt.

— *Wooden quiver*

READY FOR THE CHASE
Some African peoples use large, metal-tipped spears for hunting. These are more powerful than the San's small bow.

Bow is about 60 cm (2 ft) long

Spare arrow tip

Wooden shaft without tip

Poison quill-tipped arrow

Poison quill-tipped arrow

Metal-tipped arrow

STRAIGHTENER
This grooved stone is heated and pressed along a fresh reed to form a straight arrowshaft.

THE POWER OF POISON
Some of these arrows have metal tips, but many have detachable poison quill-tips. The poison, made from beetle larvae, works slowly - hunters often have to follow the animals until they die.

Slate tip   Quartz tip   Iron tip   Bone tip

Metal-tipped arrow

Metal-tipped arrow

METAL-TIPPED SPEAR
The San sometimes use spears instead of bows for hunting larger animals, and also for fighting.

Gazelle

Snare wound
round twig

Noose of
twine

*Straps made from
animal's legs*

TRAPS AND SNARES
This selection of
snares and nooses
is used for trapping
small animals.

CARRYING BAG
This bag is used
for carrying
equipment such
as snares, and
the small
animals caught
in them.

ON THE RETREAT
Like the Bushmen, Zulu
warriors sometimes
used their long metal
spears for fighting.

MINIATURE BOW
With a small bow,
the poison tips of the
arrows have to do most
of the work of killing
the animal.

WEAPONS AT THE READY
This large leather bag is slung over the hunter's shoulder to
carry his bow and the wooden quiver with its arrows. The legs
of the animal are tied together to form the straps.

Tilling the soil

HUMANITY'S GREATEST-EVER ADVANCEMENT, farming first began in the Near East around 10,000 BC and spread throughout Europe during the next six thousand years. It also developed independently in other areas of the world, such as America and the Far East. The ability to grow plants and raise animals meant people could control their own sources of food rather than relying only on hunting and gathering. Farming enabled people to stay in one place all the year round and to fill a greater number of mouths. As a result the population increased and towns began to develop.

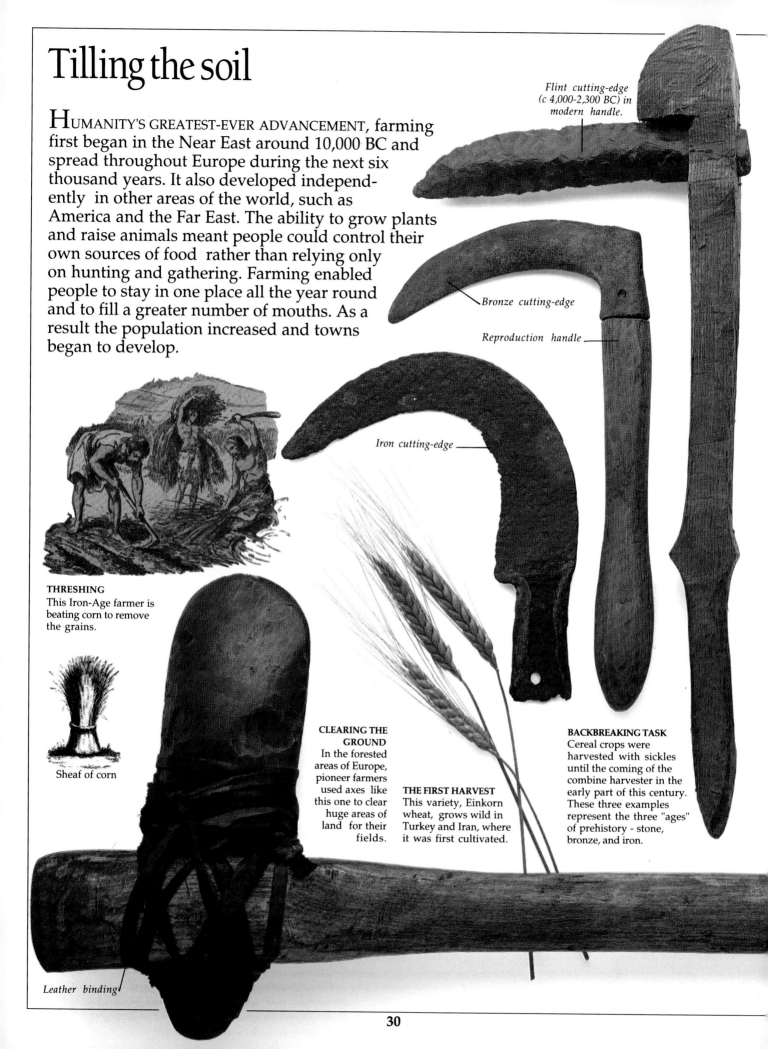

Flint cutting-edge (c 4,000-2,300 BC) in modern handle.

Bronze cutting-edge

Reproduction handle

Iron cutting-edge

THRESHING
This Iron-Age farmer is beating corn to remove the grains.

Sheaf of corn

CLEARING THE GROUND
In the forested areas of Europe, pioneer farmers used axes like this one to clear huge areas of land for their fields.

THE FIRST HARVEST
This variety, Einkorn wheat, grows wild in Turkey and Iran, where it was first cultivated.

BACKBREAKING TASK
Cereal crops were harvested with sickles until the coming of the combine harvester in the early part of this century. These three examples represent the three "ages" of prehistory - stone, bronze, and iron.

Leather binding

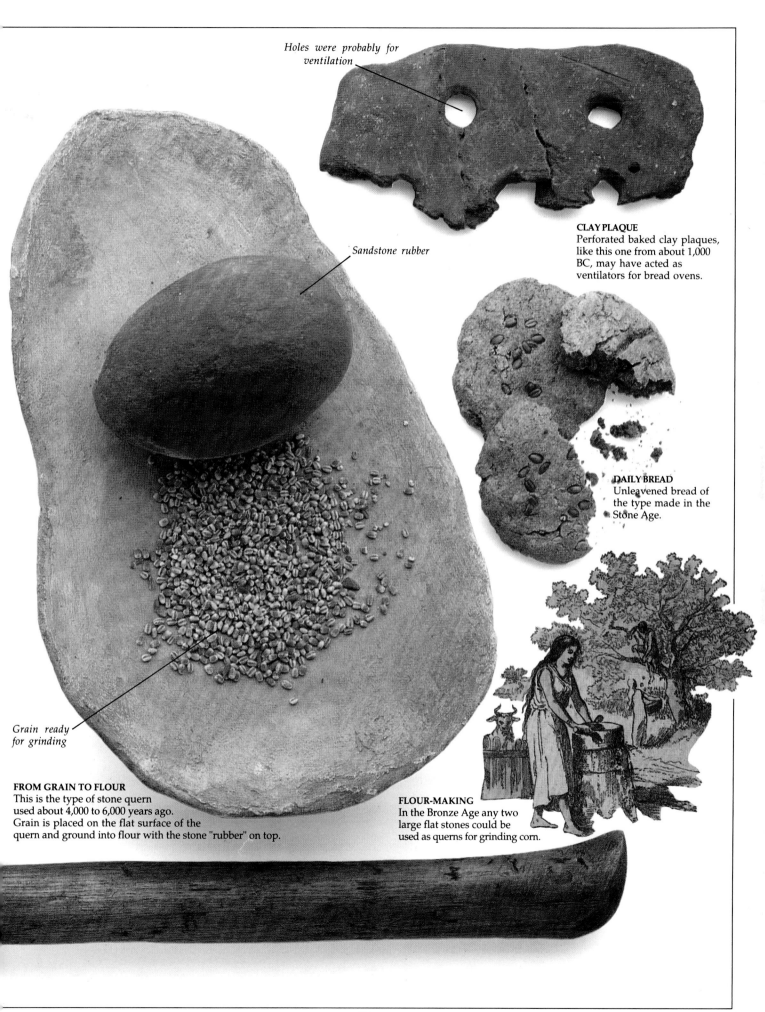

Holes were probably for
ventilation

Sandstone rubber

CLAY PLAQUE
Perforated baked clay plaques,
like this one from about 1,000
BC, may have acted as
ventilators for bread ovens.

DAILY BREAD
Unleavened bread of
the type made in the
Stone Age.

Grain ready
for grinding

FROM GRAIN TO FLOUR
This is the type of stone quern
used about 4,000 to 6,000 years ago.
Grain is placed on the flat surface of the
quern and ground into flour with the stone "rubber" on top.

FLOUR-MAKING
In the Bronze Age any two
large flat stones could be
used as querns for grinding corn.

Clothing and fabrics

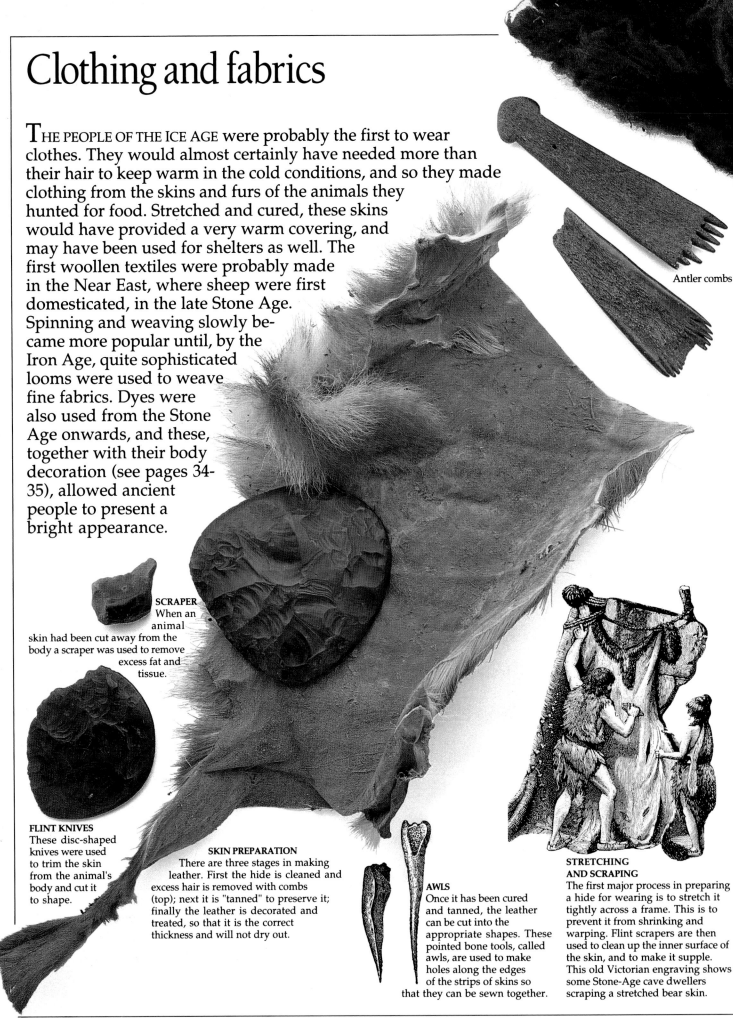

THE PEOPLE OF THE ICE AGE were probably the first to wear clothes. They would almost certainly have needed more than their hair to keep warm in the cold conditions, and so they made clothing from the skins and furs of the animals they hunted for food. Stretched and cured, these skins would have provided a very warm covering, and may have been used for shelters as well. The first woollen textiles were probably made in the Near East, where sheep were first domesticated, in the late Stone Age. Spinning and weaving slowly became more popular until, by the Iron Age, quite sophisticated looms were used to weave fine fabrics. Dyes were also used from the Stone Age onwards, and these, together with their body decoration (see pages 34-35), allowed ancient people to present a bright appearance.

Antler combs

SCRAPER When an animal skin had been cut away from the body a scraper was used to remove excess fat and tissue.

FLINT KNIVES
These disc-shaped knives were used to trim the skin from the animal's body and cut it to shape.

SKIN PREPARATION
There are three stages in making leather. First the hide is cleaned and excess hair is removed with combs (top); next it is "tanned" to preserve it; finally the leather is decorated and treated, so that it is the correct thickness and will not dry out.

AWLS
Once it has been cured and tanned, the leather can be cut into the appropriate shapes. These pointed bone tools, called awls, are used to make holes along the edges of the strips of skins so that they can be sewn together.

STRETCHING AND SCRAPING
The first major process in preparing a hide for wearing is to stretch it tightly across a frame. This is to prevent it from shrinking and warping. Flint scrapers are then used to clean up the inner surface of the skin, and to make it supple. This old Victorian engraving shows some Stone-Age cave dwellers scraping a stretched bear skin.

RAW WOOL
In ancient times the raw wool was simply plucked off the back of the sheep when it was moulting.

Spun wool

Spindle whorl

SPINDLE
The raw wool is twisted round and round the wooden spindle to make a single thread. The clay spindle whorl on the end provides a weight to help the spinning motion.

SPINNING AND WEAVING
This old engraving shows two of the main processes in wool production. The woman in the foreground is spinning the raw wool on the tree into a single thread by twining it round a spindle in her left hand. The man in the background is using a loom to weave the vertical and horizontal threads.

Safflower yellow

Safflower red

WOOL DYES
The safflower, or dyer's thistle, has been used since 2,000 BC.

ANCIENT WOOL
This wool comes from a species of wild sheep which now lives only on the Isle of Soay in the Hebrides, off Scotland. It gives us a good idea of what ancient wool looked like. The brown colour is quite natural. This wool has then been spun into a single thread and is now ready to be knitted or woven into a garment or container.

Neolithic textile

Hole for suspension

LOOM
The loom, first invented in the late Stone Age, made it possible to produce woven fabrics for the first time. The frame stretches the vertical woollen threads, and a shuttle is used to weave the horizontal threads in between them.

Recent American backstrap loom

Bone shuttle

Clay loomweight for stretching threads

Skin deep

In the past, most people decorated their bodies much more than we do in the West today. Tomb paintings, sculptures, and preserved bodies give us some idea of the kinds of ornament used by peoples of the past, and we can glean more information from looking at recent non-Western cultures. The types of decoration used range from tattooing and body-painting to elaborate hairstyling and the wearing of jewellery by both men and women.

THE POWER OF PAINTING
North American Indian medicine men sometimes used elaborate body painting when imitating evil spirits

SEEING RED
Red pigment (rouge), kept in this box from southern New Guinea, may be applied just to the face or all over the body.

UNLIKELY PERFUME
Ambergris comes from the intestines of sperm whales. It is strong-smelling and was used as a basis for scents in the islands of the South Pacific.

FOR BAD BREATH
The resin from a type of spruce tree, frankincense was used to sweeten the breath.

Face paint

Seed pods

FACE PAINT
This lump of red face paint and the seed pods from which it was made come from Gran Chaco, South America.

Spoon and spatula for preparing kohl for use as make-up

Ground pigments

EYE MAKE-UP
These blocks were ground into a powder, called kohl. It was used for darkening the skin around the eyes.

HAIR COMB
People of the Amazon rain forest used decorated combs like this.

BLACK AND BEAUTIFUL
This carved coconut contains noti, a mixture for blackening the teeth. It comes from the Solomon Islands.

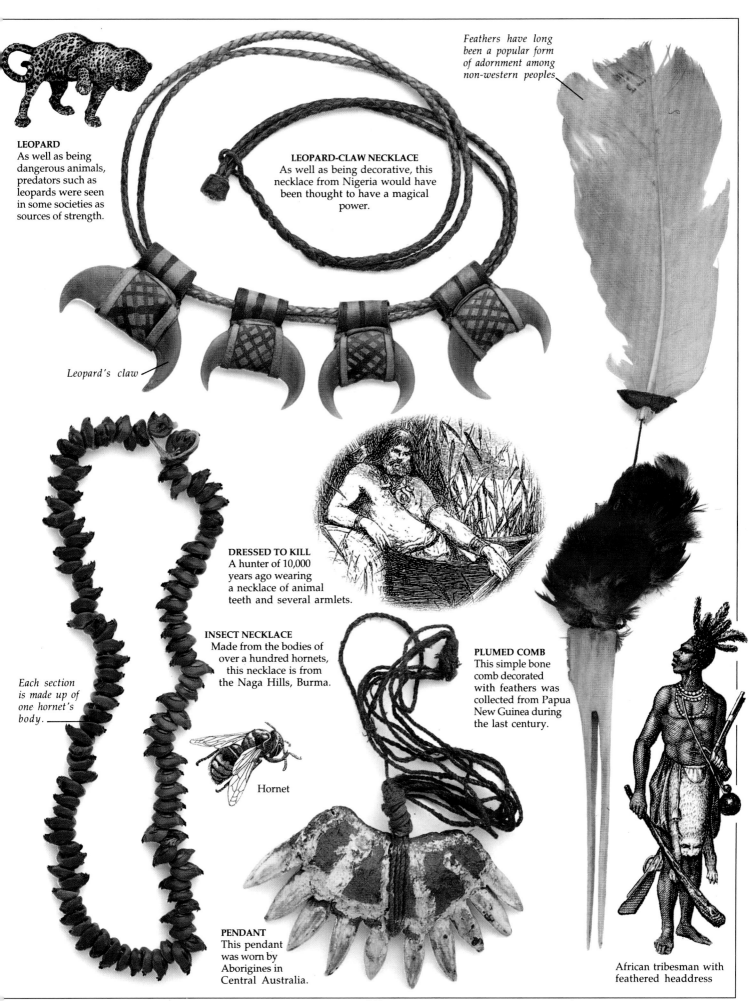

LEOPARD
As well as being dangerous animals, predators such as leopards were seen in some societies as sources of strength.

LEOPARD-CLAW NECKLACE
As well as being decorative, this necklace from Nigeria would have been thought to have a magical power.

Feathers have long been a popular form of adornment among non-western peoples

Leopard's claw

DRESSED TO KILL
A hunter of 10,000 years ago wearing a necklace of animal teeth and several armlets.

INSECT NECKLACE
Made from the bodies of over a hundred hornets, this necklace is from the Naga Hills, Burma.

Each section is made up of one hornet's body.

Hornet

PLUMED COMB
This simple bone comb decorated with feathers was collected from Papua New Guinea during the last century.

PENDANT
This pendant was worn by Aborigines in Central Australia.

African tribesman with feathered headdress

Magic

AMONG SMALL-SCALE, non-scientific societies, magic and witchcraft are an essential part of everyday life. In such a world it is quite natural to believe that misfortunes such as illness and accidents are caused by powers which take the form of spirits. It is also understandable that people believe that they must consult the spirits in order to find out why some evil has occurred, and what can be done to remedy it. Sometimes it is the job of a particular person - known as a shaman, diviner, or witch doctor - to do this. Usually some sort of offering will need to be made or a ritual performed. Charms are also often worn to protect the wearer from evil. It is likely that the very earliest humans practised magic, using it to tell them the best times and places to hunt and the best ways to cure illnesses, but little evidence survives. Most of the objects shown here are therefore from recent societies.

THE DEVIL'S DANCE
This shaman is performing the devil's dance, a religious ceremony of the west coast of Africa. Elaborate costumes, imitating animals or birds, are a common feature of such ceremonies.

FOR FERTILITY
These objects, made of a substance called faience, are Egyptian fertility symbols.

This African shaman is using a snake and some bones to foretell the future.

Cowrie shells

CHARMS *right and below*
In ancient societies it was a common practice to wear charms (sometimes called "amulets"), to guard against harm. These took many shapes, but were often worn around the wrist, like the charm bracelets of today.

Cowrie-shell charm from the Mojave-Apache Indians

Bead bracelet from Northern India

SACRED BUNDLE
Collected in Uganda, this leather bundle is covered with cowrie shells. It originally contained various sacred objects used by a diviner.

POWERFUL POPPY
The narcotic effects of opium poppy seeds have been known for thousands of years. In some societies witch doctors used drugs like this to produce trances.

Piece of wood that was floated on the water in the bowl

BELLS
In many cases divining is done in a trance-like state, to the accompaniment of music and dancing. Drums are used, and bells, like these goat bells from Tanzania are sometimes rung continuously.

DIVINING BOWL
Divining bowls help find out causes of misfortune. This one from Tanzania was filled with water. Objects were then floated on the surface and the shaman interpreted their movements.

Nutshells

A huge stilt-walking figure in the Apono giant dance

FOR GOOD HEALTH
This little red figure is made up of a combination of wood, bone, leather, cloth, and nuts. It was used amongst the Nte'va people of the Upper Congo "to watch one's body", in other words to protect them from illness.

DIRECT LINE TO THE SPIRITS
Diviners communicate with a spirit in different ways. Some read messages, some become possessed by the spirit itself, and others speak directly to it through sacred objects like this antelope horn from central Africa.

FISH CHARM
This amulet was worn round the neck as a charm against evil spirits. It was collected in Papua New Guinea and is in the form of a local snapping fish inside a basket.

Death and burial

SINCE THE FIRST Neanderthal burials about 40,000 years ago (see pages 18-19), most people have disposed of their dead formally - by burial, cremation, or mummification. For most of them, death was not the end of their existence, but one stage in a journey. Death has often been seen as the time when the spirit leaves the body to live elsewhere - in heaven, in the landscape, in a tomb, or simply in the household. So in ancient societies, as now, death was looked on as an important stage in a person's existence, and was marked with ceremonies. The treatment of the dead varied greatly from society to society, and was often a complicated procedure. In some ancient societies, a funeral pyre was built and the dead person cremated with sacrificial victims. The bones might then be housed in a burial chamber with rich offerings to accompany the individual in the afterlife. Because such burials were performed deliberately, they are often very well preserved. By study of burial remains, archaeologists can tell quite a lot about the treatment of the dead in a particular ancient society, and deduce something about the living society too.

AN EARLY BURIAL
This reconstruction shows the burial of a woman in front of a cave at Les Eyzies, France. The site dates from around 12,000-9,000 BC.

The entrance to a chambered tomb, the Cairn of Dowth, Ireland

THE PYRAMIDS
This royal cemetery, containing some of the most famous tombs in the world, was built between 2,700 and 2,500 BC. The three largest pyramids contained the pharaohs Khufu, Khafra, and Menkaura.

Mummy pits are visible in the foreground

HOUSES OF THE DEAD
"Megaliths" is the name given to a group of monuments consisting of huge slabs of stone. Some of them seem never to have housed human remains, but were simply monuments, while others contained the remains of scores of jumbled-up skeletons. These examples are around five thousand years old.

Barley

FOOD FOR THE DEAD
These seeds from the burial of the Egyptian pharaoh Tutankhamun were recently found in an old box at Kew Gardens, England. They had been recovered during excavation and sent for analysis, but lay forgotten for 46 years. They are the remains of food offerings, and tell us much about the plants and diet available at the time.

Jujubes

Melon   Mimusops

Cremation urn

A megalith consisting of six uprights and a covering slab, at Gaulstown, Ireland

BURIAL MOUND
This engraving shows a skeleton from c 2,000 BC buried in a chamber covered by a stone slab. Above it, a cremation in an urn has been buried at a later date.

This type of pot was often used both in the home and in cremations.

Mummification

Although we usually associate mummies with the Egyptians, they also occur in other areas of the world. In certain parts of coastal Peru, dry desert conditions have helped to preserve bodies almost complete, with their hair and all the usually perishable grave offerings.

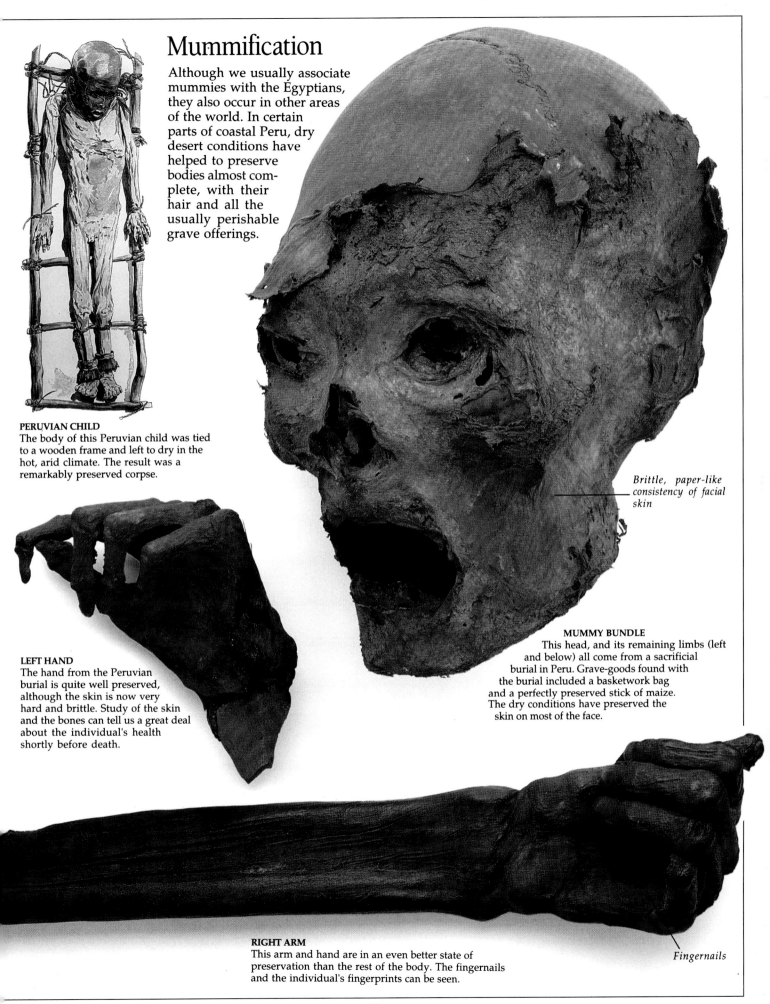

PERUVIAN CHILD
The body of this Peruvian child was tied to a wooden frame and left to dry in the hot, arid climate. The result was a remarkably preserved corpse.

LEFT HAND
The hand from the Peruvian burial is quite well preserved, although the skin is now very hard and brittle. Study of the skin and the bones can tell us a great deal about the individual's health shortly before death.

Brittle, paper-like consistency of facial skin

MUMMY BUNDLE
This head, and its remaining limbs (left and below) all come from a sacrificial burial in Peru. Grave-goods found with the burial included a basketwork bag and a perfectly preserved stick of maize. The dry conditions have preserved the skin on most of the face.

RIGHT ARM
This arm and hand are in an even better state of preservation than the rest of the body. The fingernails and the individual's fingerprints can be seen.

Fingernails

Ancient writing

THE FIRST WRITING gradually developed in Mesopotamia (in part of modern Iraq) and was used to record trading deals. At first, pictures of the objects being exchanged were simply drawn on tokens; later, symbols were used to represent ideas. By about 3,500 BC, the actual sounds of speech (either whole words or syllables) were written down on clay tablets using a stylus. This type of script is known as cuneiform. The idea of writing spread around the Old World, and by around 1,000 BC the Phoenicians had invented an alphabet. Writing was also independently invented in other places. In China it first appears engraved on bones to record military affairs and the deeds of kings. In Central America, the Maya used hieroglyphs, most of which have only recently been deciphered, to make astronomical records and list kingly dynasties. In all these ancient societies writing was restricted to the elite because it was a source of knowledge and power.

CUNEIFORM TABLET
The earliest form of writing, known as cuneiform, consists of signs made by pressing a wedge-ended stylus into a slab of wet clay. This is an account table from Mesopotamia, dating from c 3,400 BC.

FOUNDATION STONE
This four-thousand-year-old brick cone, from the famous Sumerian city of Ur, was placed in a mudbrick wall to record the foundation of a building.

Cuneiform signs made with a wedge-ended stylus

Seal

Impression

Seal

Impression

Seal

CYLINDER SEAL
This was used in early Mesopotamia to seal documents. Cylinder seals bore the name of their owner, and were simply rolled over the moist clay of a tablet to make a distinctive impression. This one is over 5,000 years old.

BOAR SEAL *left*
Seals were made from a variety of stones, some of them precious, and had a number of different forms. This one, dating from about 3,400 BC, takes the form of a wild boar.

BULL SEAL *right*
The great Indus civilization of northern India and Pakistan reached its peak between 2,300 and 1,750 BC. Like the Sumerians, the Indus people also used a form of writing, and recorded trading deals with seals. This stone seal, showing a bull, is typical of the period.

Seal

Impression

Mayan writing
stamped on
pottery

Mayan writing
engraved on bone

Painted
Mayan
writing

MAYAN WRITING
For generations,
scholars were baffled by
the pictorial script of the
Maya. It bears no resemblance to
any other known writing. The first
simple bars and dots of the calendar
were translated in 1880, but for nearly a
hundred years it was thought that Mayan
writing was used only for recording the
calendar and for astronomical calculations. It
was not till the 1960s that researchers found that
some glyphs referred to the kings and their exploits.
Now nearly 80 per cent are deciphered and a history
of the Maya is being uncovered.

Mayan characters

MAYAN TOMB SLAB *above*
The writing on this stone relief
identifies it as showing the ruler
"Shield Jaguar" with his wife, Lady
Xoc, kneeling before him and ritually
drawing blood from her tongue.

Writing in Egypt

The idea of writing probably travelled
to Egypt from western Asia, but the
script itself was invented locally.
Three basic kinds were used. The
official script used for inscriptions is
hieroglyphic; for writing on papyrus
with pens, priests used a form called
hieratic; a simpler kind, called de-
motic, was for everyday use.

人
Man

二
Two

上
On

富
Rich

CHINESE CHARACTERS *above*
The Chinese script is the oldest writing still in
use in the world. In the Bronze-Age Shang
period a form was used from around 1,300 BC
which is still recognizably related to modern
Chinese. In 221 BC the Ch'in state brought in a
standard script to replace all the regional
variations that had grown up, and this is still
used today.

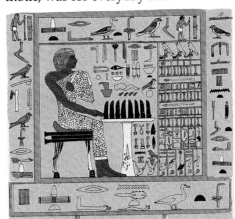

SCRIBES AT WORK *above*
Armies of scribes were vital
to the functioning of Ancient
Egypt's complex society.
They ensured records were
kept, business was
conducted, and taxes
collected.

HIEROGLYPHICS *left*
Hieroglyphic is a kind
of script where the
symbols stand for parts
of words. It was
developed about 3,000
BC and, unlike cuneiform,
was used for historical
records, especially on
tombs and temples.

PAPYRUS *above*
Early paper was made
from this reed.

Bronzeworking

BRONZE IS A MIXTURE of copper and tin. Its use became widespread in Europe around 2,000 BC. Copper had been used to make metal objects before this date, but these were usually only ornamental because both metals are too soft to make useful tools or weapons. By adding ten per cent tin to the copper, a far harder alloy could be produced, and one which could be cast in many different shapes. It could also take a sharp edge and be resharpened or melted down and recast when it was worn. All these qualities made it a very useful metal indeed.Most bronze objects (from swords to brooches, knives to pins) were made by casting - pouring the molten metal into a mould and allowing it to cool and set. Sheet-metal items such as shields were hammered into shape. While stone is abundant locally, copper ores are not common in Europe, and tin ores are rare, so the change brought with it widespread social changes. Prospectors and miners appeared, long-distance trade in metal ingots developed, and central trading areas came into being. Control of the trade was a great source of power, and large fortified settlements grew up which dominated the trade routes and served as centres of manufacturing.

MELTING DOWN THE ORE
Copper and tin, the usual ingredients of bronze, occur as ores which have to be mined from the earth. In order to obtain the metal, the ore is heated to a high temperature to melt the metal and separate it from the rock. This process is known as smelting. To produce bronze, solid copper and tin ingots are melted together to form a bronze ingot. This in turn can be remelted and poured into a mould.

A PRECIOUS METAL
When casting objects in bronze, the hot metal had to be handled carefully. The crucible was held with a long handle as the metal was poured into the mould. The skill required to cast objects in this way, together with the specialist equipment needed, made bronze items particularly valuable. People had to be prepared to barter with the bronzeworker to obtain the things they wanted.

BRONZE DEBRIS
When copper and tin ores are melted together, the resulting alloy is collected in the bottom of the crucible in bowl-shaped ingots. The piece of debris to the left shows part of the outline of one of these.

Long blade for "slashing" action

Original golden colour

STONE MOULD
This is one section of a two-piece mould used for casting spherical-headed pins. When the two halves were joined togehter, molten bronze was poured in through holes at the pointed end of each pin. This mould is from Mörigen, Switzerland, and dates from c 1000 BC.

PINS
Bronzeworkers were capable of producing quite elaborately decorated objects, as these pins from Switzerland show. The different types of patterns on pins like this can give archaeologists useful clues as to the origins of bronze items and the people who made them.

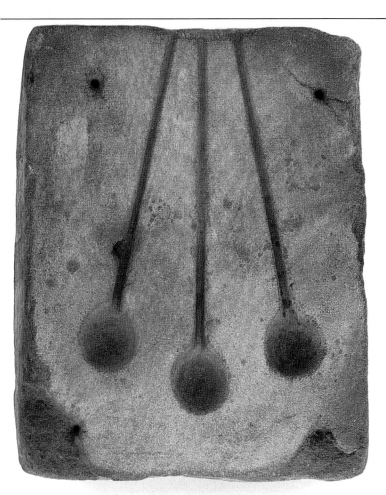

END PRODUCT
This is the type of bronze pin that would have been produced using the stone mould shown.

READY FOR RECYCLING
These axes, dating from c 750 BC, are damaged. They may have formed part of the stock-in-trade of a bronzeworker, ready to melt down and recycle.

MOMENT OF TRUTH
These bronzeworkers are casting swords with similar-shaped handles to the one shown below. The person in the foreground is examining a sword to check that it is free of flaws. The mould used in this process has an extra channel through which to pour in the metal. When the cast has set and the mould was opened up, the excess bronze found in this channel was removed. Extra metal where the two halves of the mould joined together was also removed or smoothed down.

Decorated hilt

TWO SWORDS
These swords would have been cast using the methods shown on this page. The upper sword is from Avignon, France and the lower is from Denmark. The Danish sword has been cleaned to show its original gold colour, whereas the French sword is the dull , uncleaned colour of most ancient bronze objects.

The beauties of bronze

BRONZE TOOLS AND WEAPONS are not much sharper than flint ones, so the original reason for developing bronzeworking around 2,000 BC was probably to do with social status. When it is new, bronze is a shiny gold colour and can be richly decorated. It soon became a valuable substance, and one which was ideally suited for showing a person's wealth and power. When it was first invented it was popular amongst the aristocracy for ornamental objects such as jewellery, as well as being used to make tools and weapons, which themselves were often impressively decorated. When iron became widespread in Europe, around 750 BC, it was used for the heavier tools and weapons, thus freeing the bronze-workers to concentrate on producing luxury items and decorative objects, like jewellery, ornaments, and horse harness decorations.

WHAT ARE THEY DOING?
This mysterious engraving is taken from the design on a bronze vessel found in the Tyrol, Austria.

HORSEMANSHIP
In the late Bronze Age the use of horses became widespread.

PENDANT
This beaten bronze pendant was probably suspended on a chain worn around the neck. The type of simple bronze chain in use at this time is shown on the opposite page.

Pin is shown actual size

Harness mounts found in Norfolk, England

TWEEZERS
Like today, tweezers were probably used in the Bronze Age for pulling out hairs.

Typical serpentine ornament

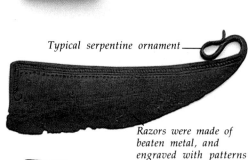

Razors were made of beaten metal, and engraved with patterns

BRIDLE SIDE-PIECE
This part of a horse harness was found in Cambridge, England.

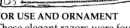

RICHES OF THE CELTS
The chariots of the aristocratic Celtic horsemen of the late Iron Age (c 100 BC-AD 100) were decorated with fine metalwork. Here, red enamel highlights the pattern.

FOR USE AND ORNAMENT
These elegant razors were found in Denmark. Human bodies, preserved in the peat in the same area, were clean shaven, and no doubt used razors similar to these.

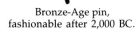

Bronze-Age pin, fashionable after 2,000 BC.

Fastening held closed
by tension of ring

SUNFLOWER PINS
These pins are so named
because of the position
of their carefully
crafted heads, which
would have shone
brightly on the
clothing of their
wearer. They date
from c 1200 BC.

WORN BY THE POWERFUL
The neck ring or "torc"
was an important status
symbol in the Celtic-
speaking world of the
Iron Age. Torcs were
also worn by warriors
as a protective charm.
This one, from the 6th
century BC, is made
from a single piece of
twisted bronze.

*Flower-
shaped
head*

AROUND THE WAIST
One of a series of ornaments
attached to a belt, this boss was
made from a thin sheet of bronze.
The decorations were hammered
upward from the back, using a
technique called *repoussé*. This boss
is from Auvernier, Switzerland.

Simple bent-metal link

SWISS JEWELLERY
This chain may have
formed part of a
necklace. It was found
in a Bronze-Age
village by an Alpine
lake.

Found in Denmark, this
is the pattern for a
woman's jacket.

WOMEN'S BELT BOSS
These bosses have been found
with many female burials in Denmark.

BRACELET
Some of the richest
bracelets from the Bronze
Age took the form of metal
spirals.

ALL DRESSED UP
Bronze-Age women would have worn dresses
like the one shown in this engraving.

A Bronze-Age warrior

THROUGHOUT THE WESTERN WORLD a more obviously warlike society was evolving around 2,200-700 BC, the time of the Bronze Age in Europe. This period gives us our first evidence of individual armed combat, and of societies in which the warrior and his skills were highly valued. The weapons used were spears, for attacking enemies at a distance, and swords and axes, proving that hand-to-hand fighting took place. The high position of warriors during the Bronze Age is shown by the richness of their personal ornaments (which included jewellery such as bangles and pins with large ornate heads) and the elaborate decoration on some of their weapons.

BANGLE
This intricately engraved bangle is from Auvernier, Switzerland and dates from c 1,200 BC

Found in Switzerland, these pins date from c 1,000 BC

BEFORE BUTTONS
Pins were used for fastening clothing before the invention of buttons.

STATUS SYMBOLS
Spears were symbols of the warrior in the Bronze Age, and were often very ornate.

FOR FOOD OR FIGHTING?
Small knives, like this one from Switzerland, were probably used for cutting food rather than as weapons.

THE FIRST KNIGHTS
Horse-riding became widespread in the late Bronze Age, and men used slashing swords for fighting.

CEREMONIAL SPEARHEAD
Together with its wooden shaft, this massive socketed spearhead from Hungary would have made a weapon over 2m (6 ft) long. It was almost certainly for ceremonial use rather than for actual use in battle.

LIGHTWEIGHT SPEAR
This small spear tip is from Amiens, France. The spear would have been thrown at the enemy like a javelin.

Socket for wooden shaft

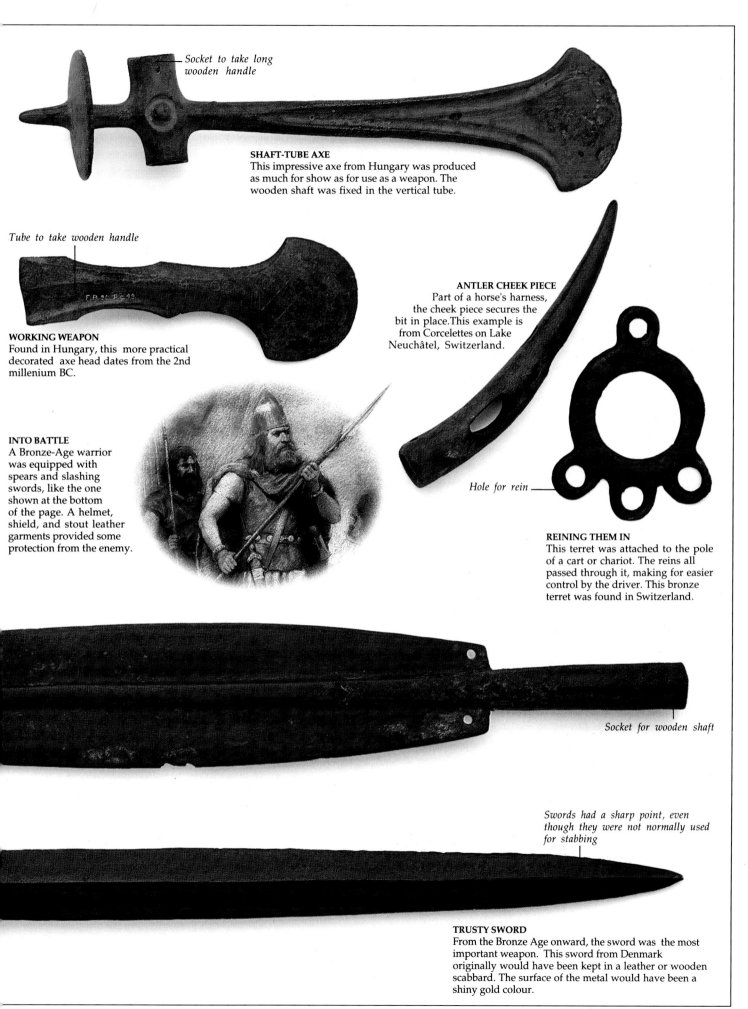

Socket to take long wooden handle

SHAFT-TUBE AXE
This impressive axe from Hungary was produced as much for show as for use as a weapon. The wooden shaft was fixed in the vertical tube.

Tube to take wooden handle

WORKING WEAPON
Found in Hungary, this more practical decorated axe head dates from the 2nd millenium BC.

ANTLER CHEEK PIECE
Part of a horse's harness, the cheek piece secures the bit in place. This example is from Corcelettes on Lake Neuchâtel, Switzerland.

INTO BATTLE
A Bronze-Age warrior was equipped with spears and slashing swords, like the one shown at the bottom of the page. A helmet, shield, and stout leather garments provided some protection from the enemy.

Hole for rein

REINING THEM IN
This terret was attached to the pole of a cart or chariot. The reins all passed through it, making for easier control by the driver. This bronze terret was found in Switzerland.

Socket for wooden shaft

Swords had a sharp point, even though they were not normally used for stabbing

TRUSTY SWORD
From the Bronze Age onward, the sword was the most important weapon. This sword from Denmark originally would have been kept in a leather or wooden scabbard. The surface of the metal would have been a shiny gold colour.

Iron-Age finery

SOME OF THE FINEST decorated personal items of the Iron Age are made of bronze, because iron was reserved for heavy tools and weapons. Unlike iron, bronze could be cast into complex shapes and be highly decorated. Classical writers report that the Celts of Iron Age Europe were fond of adornment, including body painting, elaborate hairstyles, and jewellery (see pages 34-35). A characteristic ornament was a silver neck ring called a torc, symbolic of high social rank. Some fighting men went into battle naked except for their torc, trusting in its protective power. Over their trousers and tunics men and women wore woollen cloaks fastened with brooches, sometimes of elaborate design. In graves, it is usually only these that survive to indicate the sort of clothing that was worn. The aristocracy would adorn their horses with fine harnesses covered with discs, studs, and bells.

SPECTACLE-BROOCH
This type of brooch is so called because of its shape. It is made from a single twisted piece of wire and would have had a pin at the back. It is from Carinthia in Austria and dates from between 1,000 and 800 BC.

Pin

Spring

SAFETY PIN
Brooches were the prehistoric equivalents of safety pins. They were used in exactly the same way as nowadays, for joining clothes together. This Hungarian brooch dates from c 50 BC.

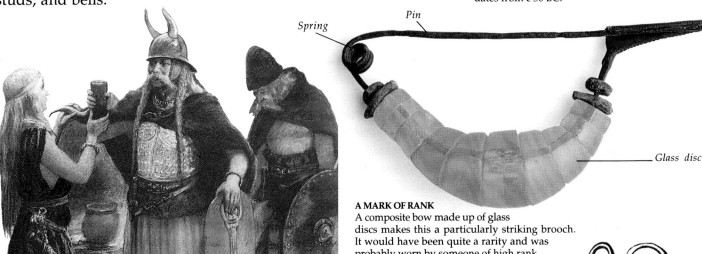

Pin

Spring

Glass disc

A MARK OF RANK
A composite bow made up of glass discs makes this a particularly striking brooch. It would have been quite a rarity and was probably worn by someone of high rank. It is from Italy, and dates from between 800 and 700 BC.

CHIEFTAIN
In this rather romantic engraving, the nineteenth-century illustrator has tried to combine all the elements known about Iron Age dress into one picture. The chieftain has a horned helmet and a bushy moustache (although pigtails are not reported!). His cloak is fastened by a brooch, and he is wearing a shiny breastplate for battle. Under his short tunic he wears trousers which are ideal for horse-riding. The woman has an elaborate girdle, from which a dagger hangs. She is presenting the chieftain with a drinking horn filled with beer taken from the decorated pail in the foreground.

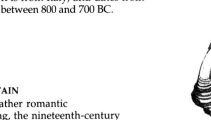

FIRM FASTENINGS
Two more examples from northern Europe show the skill that Iron-Age metalworkers could lavish on these simple fasteners. The strong, sprung pins themselves are clearly visible.

FOLLOWING THE PATTERN
This bronze pendant with enamelled decoration is from a Saxon burial slightly later than the other objects on this page. But the curves and circles used in its decoration show how this style of art continued to be used in northern Europe.

FOR MEN AND WOMEN
Bracelets like this were commonly worn on the arms - probably by both male and female members of the household. This one was found near Cambridge, England, and was made c 50 BC. Its delicate pattern would have been more striking when it was new.

A CLEAN SHAVE
This razor, now about 2,500 years old, is less ornate than some of the razors of the Bronze Age (see page 44-45) but it is highly functional: it would have been just as sharp as any modern cut-throat razor. It comes from Cambridge, England.

WELL SHOD
Iron-Age horse shoes are sometimes found. Their form is similar to those in use today.

Decorated back of mirror

FAIREST OF THEM ALL
Some of the most beautiful objects that have survived form the Iron Age are mirrors. This one is decorated in the distinctive, swirling style of 'Celtic' art. The back is shown in the photograph; the other side would be highly polished to give a reflection. Mirrors like this are rare and no doubt belonged to the wealthiest families.

BOAR HUNT
Iron horse shoes similar to the one above can be seen in this old engraving. The fine trappings that decorate the horses of the huntsmen are also clearly shown. The large discs are made of bronze and are known as "phalerae". In the Iron Age the boar was hunted for sport as well as for its meat.

Life in the Iron Age

THE FIRST REALLY ACCOMPLISHED IRONWORKERS were the Hittites, who lived in what is now central Turkey, and who perfected the techniques of smelting ore and making iron objects around 1,500 BC. The Hittites guarded the secrets of ironworking carefully, but when their empire was overthrown their knowledge spread across Europe, where the Iron Age began around 1,100 BC. By this time, Europe was quite densely settled with small farming communities. Although the society as a whole was dominated by a warrior aristocracy (see pages 52-53), life for most people consisted of an unending round of farming activities, essentially unchanged for generations. Settlements were still mainly family-based, and even small children would have played a full part in daily work. Many iron objects (especially tools) have survived from this period, as well as a large amount of pottery, and decorative objects made of bronze.

INSTANT PATTERNS
Later Saxon potters made similar shaped pots to those of the Iron Age, but decorated them with punches.

Punch for cross pattern

Punch for circle pattern

BOG PEOPLE
Bodies preserved in the airless conditions of European peat bogs give us a glimpse of the actual people of the Iron Age. Tollund Man, discovered in Denmark, dates from about 210 BC.

BRONZE BOWL
In the Iron Age many of the more decorative and high-status objects were in fact made of bronze, a material that looked shiny and could be engraved with elaborate patterns. Fine bronze imported tableware like this bowl was highly prized by many aristocratic families in northern Europe, who were eager to adopt Mediterranean customs.

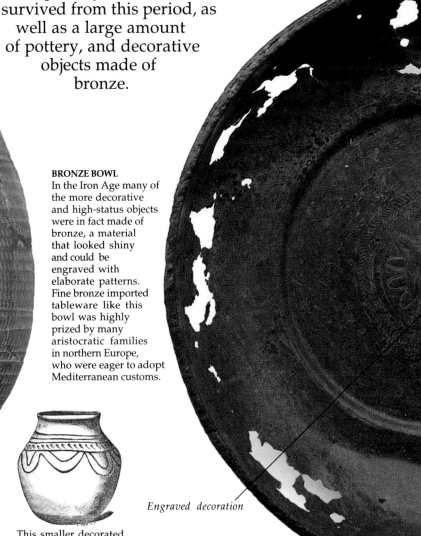

Engraved decoration

Shape made by hammering out bronze

This smaller decorated pot was found in a British Iron-Age burial mound.

STATUS SYMBOL?
In the last hundred years before the Roman invasion of Britain, wealthy people developed a taste for fine pottery. Beakers like this one were imported from Europe in large numbers.

IRON TOOLS

The introduction of iron into Europe provided an ideal material for making sturdy tools and weapons; iron was also more widely available than the tin and copper needed to make bronze. Unfortunately, iron corrodes much more quickly than bronze, so most of the items that have survived are in poorer condition than bronze objects of the same period.

Iron blade

Iron blade

Antler handle

KNIFE

This small iron-bladed knife has a handle made of antler. Although the blade is corroded, the handle is very well preserved because of favourable soil conditions.

Antler handle

Serrated cutting edge

HARVESTER

This reaping hook has the same sickle-shaped design that was used for gathering hay or crops throughout the prehistoric period (see pages 30-31). This example has an antler handle.

Holes for attaching wooden handle

CUTTER

A wooden handle would originally have made this iron saw almost as easy to use as its modern counterpart.

TONGS

Iron was worked by beating it into shape while it was red hot. The metal was held in large tongs, like these from Norfolk, England.

FORGING AHEAD

In this old engraving of blacksmiths at work, the method of shaping a piece of hot metal by hammering is clearly shown. In the background, more iron is being heated in a furnace.

Men of iron

LANCE-HEAD
This unusually shaped object is made of wrought iron.

WE KNOW ABOUT the Celtic-speaking peoples who lived north of the Alps from about 500 BC through the reports of Greek and Roman historians. They describe barbarian people with customs quite different from their own, such as human sacrifice and head-hunting. These tribes were ruled by warriors, who placed a high value on their heroic lifestyle, which included feasting and drinking, reciting poetry, singing, horseriding, and, of course, skill in battle. The Celts were as concerned with scaring their enemies as with actually fighting them. We know this because of the fearsome appearance of their arms, armour, and other possessions.

Human head

A nineteenth-century illustration of a Celtic warrior chief in battle

HEAD IN HAND
The handle of this dagger is shaped like a human figure. It dates from c 100 BC-AD 100.

LETHAL LONDONER
This is a fine early dagger from c 500 BC, found in the River Thames, England.

SHINY SHEATH
Made from thin sheets of bronze riveted together, this sheath has a birch-bark lining.

HELMET FOR A HERO
This bronze helmet would have belonged to a high-ranking warrior, and was probably for display rather than battle.

Victorian illustration of Iron-Age warfare

Hollow horn made of riveted sheet bronze

Oak lining

Diameter of tankard is about 175 mm (7 in)

Loops for fastening leather interior

AXLE HUB
This decoration was attached to the axle of a light chariot of the type used against the Roman army invading Britain.

WHAT YOUR RIGHT ARM IS FOR...
Drinking was popular with the warriors, as this 2.3 litre (4 pint) bronze vessel shows. The drink was probably a beer made from barley.

BRONZE TERRET
This was fixed to the yoke of a chariot (see p. 46).

BIT BETWEEN THE TEETH
The bit is inserted in the horse's mouth and controlled by pulling on the reins. It has an iron core covered with decorated bronze.

IRON SWORD *below*
This sword would have had a decorated sheath of leather or wood. It dates from c 150 BC-AD 50.

Hilt would have been covered in wood, bone or leather

Ancient China

For thousands of years, Chinese civilization evolved with little or no contact with the western world, and the Chinese made several independent inventions, such as farming and writing. The first stone-using agricultural communities were followed by a variety of societies, most of which survived by farming a range of crops including rice and millet. True civilization dates from c 1500 BC with the Bronze-Age Shang Dynasty. At this time China was a loose group of states which were gradually joined together. Between 500 and 200 BC, the two principal states, Ch'u and Ch'in, battled for power. Under the victorious Ch'in and the later Han (206 BC-AD 220) an empire of 60 million people prospered. The Great Wall was built, and standard systems of writing, laws, and taxes were created.

CHINESE NOBLEMEN
These men belong to the court of Emperor Tscheu-Sin, c 1150 BC.

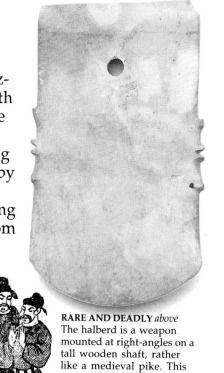

RARE AND DEADLY *above*
The halberd is a weapon mounted at right-angles on a tall wooden shaft, rather like a medieval pike. This halberd of white jade is over 3,000 years old. It was probably both for battle and for ceremonial use, especially for sacrifices.

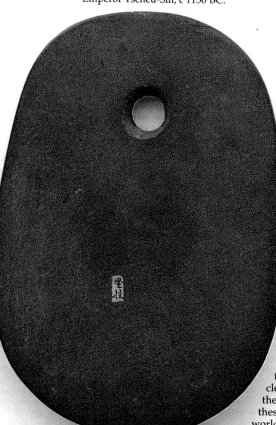

RITUAL HALBERD
This sacrificial halberd is a good example of the superb bronzeworking of the Shang Dynasty (1523-1027 BC). This skill arose from local roots, although there was also some outside influence from the west. With its ornate patterns, this halberd would have played a prominent part in rituals, for both human and animal sacrifices.

STONE TOOLS
Like their counterparts in Europe, the first Chinese farmers had to clear forests with stone axes and till the soil with mattocks. Both of these tools have similar shapes the world over. In China, however, they were used to cultivate different crops - millet in the north and rice in the south.

Stone mattock

Polished stone axe from Shansi

BRONZE AXE
This is the head of a ritual axe known as a *yüeh*, which was used for beheading human sacrifices made at funerals. These axes are often very highly decorated. The holes make the head easier to bind to the wooden shaft.

BRONZE HALBERD BLADE
The halberd was the chief weapon in ancient Chinese society. This rather simple example was used for combat. Like the other bronze halberds shown here, this one comes from the Shang dynasty (16th to 11th centuries BC).

Cutting edge

Cutting edge

THE GREAT WALL
Built between about 350 and 200 BC, the Great Wall stretches for over 2,500 miles along China's northern frontier. An army of labourers was used to build the wall, which was built to keep out nomads from Mongolia.

TERRACOTTA WARRIOR
From 246-210 BC, over 700,000 conscripts laboured over the tomb of one of China's greatest emperors, Qin Shi Huang Di. It is guarded by an army of over 7,500 terracotta warriors such as this, each one different.

Small change

WE USUALLY THINK OF MONEY as consisting of coins and banknotes, but anything used when making payments can be called money. In ancient societies many different things, from small shells to huge perforated stones, have been used to make payments, and some of these unusual types of currency continue in use today. The most common way of making a payment was originally barter, in which one item would be exchanged for another. For many societies without currency, gift-giving was very important and some valued objects were regularly passed around as gifts. Other large or rare forms of money, such as perforated stones or cattle, might be given for payments of a social kind, such as compensation for a person killed, or in exchange for a woman taken as a bride. Even after standard coinage was developed about 2,500 years ago, this social use of money continued; many examples shown here come from recent societies.

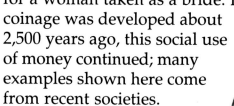

Rice

CHINESE CURRENCY
In China, coinage was invented quite independently of the Western world, but later, in the fifth century BC. The first coins looked like tiny knives; later ones were round.

Knife-shape is common in early Chinese currency

TRADE IN RICE
As well as using coinage, the Chinese used food, especially rice, to pay for different kinds of goods.

DOGS' TEETH
This necklace from Papua New Guinea is made up of the canine teeth of dogs, threaded on to a leather thong. Its function was the same as the larger one from Africa (above right).

FOR CARRYING CASH
Cowrie shells have been used as money since prehistoric times. This wicker-work purse for carrying them comes from the Congo, central Africa.

Quartz pebbles

STONE NECKLACE
This is not
simply an item
of personal jewellery:
the beads were also
used to make pay-
ments. It is made of
perforated quartz
pebbles, and comes
from Emboni in Ghana.

GAMBLING COUNTERS
Gambling is as old as money
itself, and so gambling counters
have a long history. These
decorated porcelain counters are
from Hong Kong and are nearly
2,000 years old.

*Stone is about 60 cm
(2 ft) in diameter.
The largest were up
to 4 m (13 ft) across.*

*Disc is about 23 cm
(9 in) in diameter*

Cowrie shells
from India

**TOO BIG FOR
THE POCKET**
In the
Naya hills of
Tibet, high up in
the Himalayas,
metal discs like
this were used
as currency.
Known as "laya",
this particular
example is rather
small, and had
half the value of the
more usual large size.

MONEY STONE
From Yap Island,
north of New
Guinea, lime-
stone discs
known as "fei"
were used as
currency.

DIDRACHMA
This coin is
from Aegina,
Greece. The
turtle is the sym-
bol of the city.

Central Americans

PEOPLE FIRST CAME TO AMERICA about 15,000 years ago, when hunters from Siberia followed big game across the land bridge to Alaska. These people soon began to move south and to develop without contact with the Old World. By 6,000 BC corn was being grown in Central America (in Mexico, Guatemala, El Salvador, and Belize), and gradually a number of spectacular civilizations developed. These had large ceremonial centres with temples, palaces, and markets. Many practised a ritual ball-game in specially laid-out courts. Some had an elaborate religion that included human sacrifice, and used a kind of picture-writing that is only just being understood. These civilizations were at their height between AD 300-900, after which they collapsed. They were followed by a succession of empires, such as the Aztec, the one found and overthrown by the Spanish in 1519.

WHISTLE
This whistle is made of pottery. It comes from Guatemala and is thought to represent a stylized bird.

POTTERY
This piece of decorated pottery, dating to around AD 500, comes from Teotihuacán, at the time the largest city in Mexico

CALENDAR STONE
The calendar was of great importance in the daily life of the Aztecs. Each day had its own good or evil tidings, and each month its special ceremonies. There were two different years, of 260 and 365 days, both based on a twenty-day cycle.

STONE HEAD
From Seibal in Guatemala, this sandstone head may have decorated a temple. It dates from the Classic period, AD 300-900.

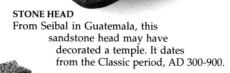

TEMPLE CARVINGS
This is a typical example of Classic period temple sculpture, showing animals, people, symbolic twisted serpents, and images of gods. It comes from a temple at Xochicalco.

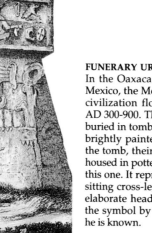

FUNERARY URN *right*
In the Oaxaca Valley of Mexico, the Monte Albán civilization flourished from AD 300-900. The dead were buried in tombs covered with brightly painted frescoes. Inside the tomb, their ashes would be housed in pottery urns such as this one. It represents a god sitting cross-legged, with an elaborate headdress containing the symbol by which he is known.

Sharp,
pointed
end

Edge shows
flintworking
of great skill

GREENSTONE MASK
The earliest Mexican civilization
was that of the Olmecs, who
occupied the Gulf coast. The Olmecs
are particularly well known for
their stone carving, and this
greenstone mask is a typical product
of their art style during the years
300 BC-AD 300.

ARCHITECTURE
The steep pyramid
temples are one of the most impressive
features of early Central American
civilizations. This old engraving
shows one that has been found
in the depths of the jungle
at Tuzapan.

MAYAN "ECCENTRIC"
This unusual flint is known as an
"eccentric" because its precise
purpose is not known. Placed in
graves as offerings, such objects
were probably prized because of
the great skill required to create
their strange and intricate shapes.

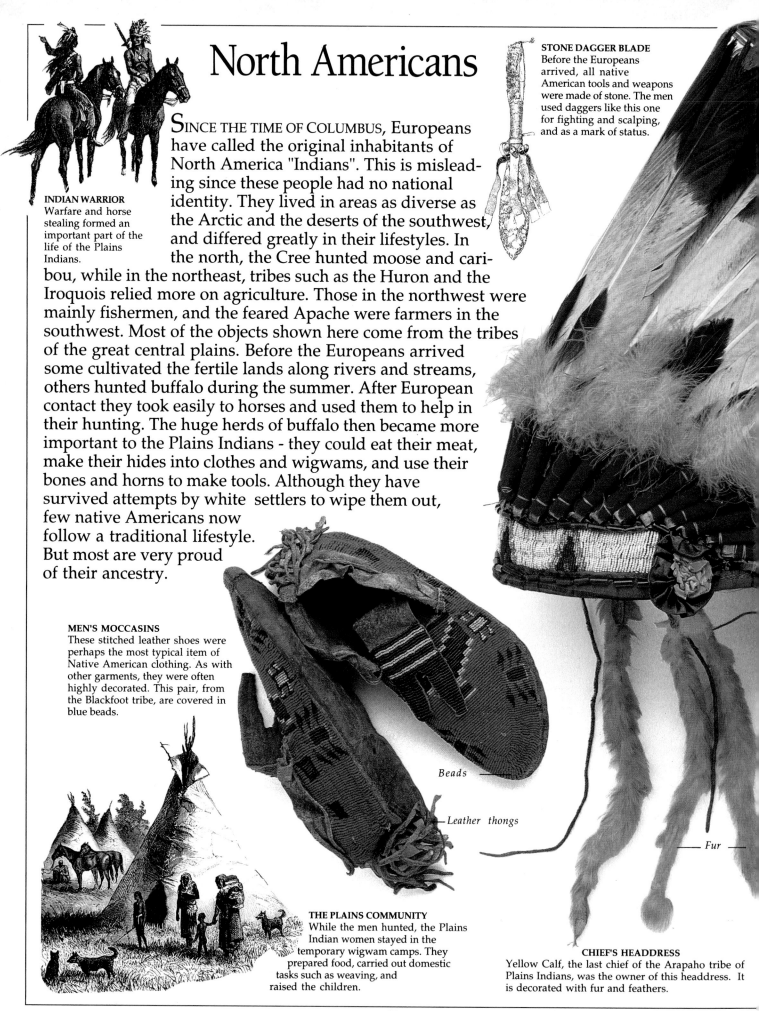

North Americans

SINCE THE TIME OF COLUMBUS, Europeans have called the original inhabitants of North America "Indians". This is misleading since these people had no national identity. They lived in areas as diverse as the Arctic and the deserts of the southwest, and differed greatly in their lifestyles. In the north, the Cree hunted moose and caribou, while in the northeast, tribes such as the Huron and the Iroquois relied more on agriculture. Those in the northwest were mainly fishermen, and the feared Apache were farmers in the southwest. Most of the objects shown here come from the tribes of the great central plains. Before the Europeans arrived some cultivated the fertile lands along rivers and streams, others hunted buffalo during the summer. After European contact they took easily to horses and used them to help in their hunting. The huge herds of buffalo then became more important to the Plains Indians - they could eat their meat, make their hides into clothes and wigwams, and use their bones and horns to make tools. Although they have survived attempts by white settlers to wipe them out, few native Americans now follow a traditional lifestyle. But most are very proud of their ancestry.

INDIAN WARRIOR
Warfare and horse stealing formed an important part of the life of the Plains Indians.

STONE DAGGER BLADE
Before the Europeans arrived, all native American tools and weapons were made of stone. The men used daggers like this one for fighting and scalping, and as a mark of status.

MEN'S MOCCASINS
These stitched leather shoes were perhaps the most typical item of Native American clothing. As with other garments, they were often highly decorated. This pair, from the Blackfoot tribe, are covered in blue beads.

Beads

Leather thongs

Fur

THE PLAINS COMMUNITY
While the men hunted, the Plains Indian women stayed in the temporary wigwam camps. They prepared food, carried out domestic tasks such as weaving, and raised the children.

CHIEF'S HEADDRESS
Yellow Calf, the last chief of the Arapaho tribe of Plains Indians, was the owner of this headdress. It is decorated with fur and feathers.

SCRAPING TOOL
Hides were prepared by scraping using a bone-handled tool with a metal blade. Earlier peoples used flints in a similar way.

Horsehair

PAINTED HIDE
This animal hide is decorated with coloured ink drawings of warriors mounted on horseback attacking bowmen with spears. The horsemen are wearing long feather headdresses. This hide is about 2 m (6 ft) long. It belonged to a group of Sioux or Crow Indians.

Feathers indicate success in hunting and war

EARTH LODGE
Some tribes built their homes by constructing a roof over a deep pit. This illustration shows such a dwelling - a Mandan earth lodge - in the nine-teenth century.

Digging up the Past

ARCHAEOLOGY PROVIDES our only means of studying most early people, since written records have only been available for a tiny fraction of our time on earth. Modern archaeology is a far cry from its old image of hunting for treasure in lost cities. Today, the archaeologist employs a whole battery of scientific techniques to help detect, excavate, and analyse the remains of ancient societies. He or she is most likely to be interested in small pieces of pottery or fragments of insects, plants, or animals, because of the information these can give about everyday life. Although archaeology is often thought of as excavation, the story only begins there. Once a "dig" is over a great deal of time is spent on analysing the material recovered, and preparing it for publication. When it is published, the notes, finds, and samples are displayed or stored in a museum.

WORKING ON SITE
Unlike the careless treasure hunting of the past, modern excavation emphasizes the meticulous vertical and horizontal recording of all features of a site. This is the excavation of an early hominid site at Sterkfontein, South Africa.

PHOTOGRAPHIC SCALES
Photographs form a vital part of the records of an excavation. These scales are essential for judging the size of the subject when it is photographed.

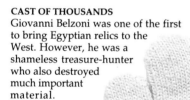

CAST OF THOUSANDS
Giovanni Belzoni was one of the first to bring Egyptian relics to the West. However, he was a shameless treasure-hunter who also destroyed much important material.

Trowel

Small, solid-forged steel blade

Paintbrush

Toothbrush

Metric scales

Cotton gloves

CLEANING
For items needing careful cleaning on site, a variety of instruments, such as these brushes, might be used.

TROWEL AND GLOVES
The trowel is the main tool used for excavation. Gloves may be used to handle delicate finds after digging.

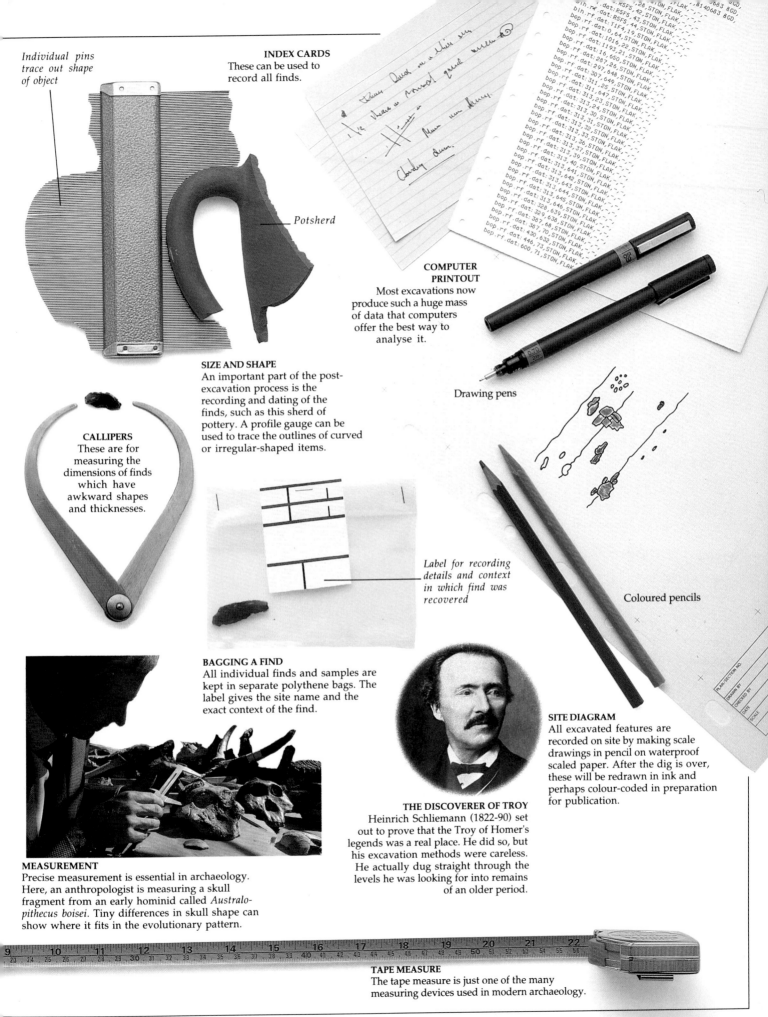

Individual pins trace out shape of object

INDEX CARDS
These can be used to record all finds.

Potsherd

bih.rf.dat: RSFS.26,STON,FLAK
bih.rf.dat: RSFS.42,STON,FLAK
bih.rf.dat: RSFS.43,STON,FLAK
bih.rf.dat: RSFS.44,STON,FLAK
bop.rf.dat: TIF4,19,STON,FLAK
bop.rf.dat: 0.64,STON,FLAK
bop.rf.dat: 1016,22,STON,FLAK
bop.rf.dat: 1193,21,STON,FLAK
bop.rf.dat: 16,650,STON,FLAK
bop.rf.dat: 287,26,STON,FLAK
bop.rf.dat: 307,649,STON,FLAK
bop.rf.dat: 311,25,STON,FLAK
bop.rf.dat: 311,647,STON,FLAK
bop.rf.dat: 313,23,STON,FLAK
bop.rf.dat: 313,24,STON,FLAK
bop.rf.dat: 313,30,STON,FLAK
bop.rf.dat: 313,31,STON,FLAK
bop.rf.dat: 313,32,STON,FLAK
bop.rf.dat: 313,33,STON,FLAK
bop.rf.dat: 313,36,STON,FLAK
bop.rf.dat: 313,37,STON,FLAK
bop.rf.dat: 313,40,STON,FLAK
bop.rf.dat: 313,641,STON,FLAK
bop.rf.dat: 313,642,STON,FLAK
bop.rf.dat: 313,644,STON,FLAK
bop.rf.dat: 313,645,STON,FLAK
bop.rf.dat: 313,646,STON,FLAK
bop.rf.dat: 329,638,STON,FLAK
bop.rf.dat: 329,639,STON,FLAK
bop.rf.dat: 387,68,STON,FLAK
bop.rf.dat: 387,70,STON,FLAK
bop.rf.dat: 430,632,STON,FLAK
bop.rf.dat: 446,73,STON,FLAK
bop.rf.dat: 600,71,STON,FLAK

COMPUTER PRINTOUT
Most excavations now produce such a huge mass of data that computers offer the best way to analyse it.

Drawing pens

SIZE AND SHAPE
An important part of the post-excavation process is the recording and dating of the finds, such as this sherd of pottery. A profile gauge can be used to trace the outlines of curved or irregular-shaped items.

CALLIPERS
These are for measuring the dimensions of finds which have awkward shapes and thicknesses.

Label for recording details and context in which find was recovered

Coloured pencils

BAGGING A FIND
All individual finds and samples are kept in separate polythene bags. The label gives the site name and the exact context of the find.

SITE DIAGRAM
All excavated features are recorded on site by making scale drawings in pencil on waterproof scaled paper. After the dig is over, these will be redrawn in ink and perhaps colour-coded in preparation for publication.

THE DISCOVERER OF TROY
Heinrich Schliemann (1822-90) set out to prove that the Troy of Homer's legends was a real place. He did so, but his excavation methods were careless. He actually dug straight through the levels he was looking for into remains of an older period.

MEASUREMENT
Precise measurement is essential in archaeology. Here, an anthropologist is measuring a skull fragment from an early hominid called *Australopithecus boisei*. Tiny differences in skull shape can show where it fits in the evolutionary pattern.

TAPE MEASURE
The tape measure is just one of the many measuring devices used in modern archaeology.

Index

Acknowledgments

Dorling Kindersley would like to thank
Peter Bailey and Lester Cheeseman for additional design assistance; Angela Murphy for additional picture research; Dr Schuyler Jones, Julia Cousins, Ray Inskeep, John Todd and John Simmonds of the Pitt-Rivers Museum, Oxford; Dr David Phillipson of the University Museum of Archaeology and Anthropology, Cambridge; Gavin Morgan of the Museum of London; Colin Keates and Chris Stringer of the Natural History Museum; the staff of the Museum of Mankind; Dave King and Jonathan Buckley; Meryl Silbert.

The following museums provided objects for photography
British Museum (Natural History), pages 6-7, 10-11, 14-15, 18-19, 22-23
Museum of London, pages 26-27, 30-31, 32-33, 46-47, 52-53, 62-63
Museum of Mankind, pages 20-21, 38-39, 60-61
Pitt-Rivers Museum, Oxford, pages 12-13, 16-17, 28-29, 34-35, 36-37, 56-57
University Museum of Archaeology and Anthropology, Cambridge, pages 24-25, 40-41, 42-43, 44-45, 48-49, 50-51, 54-55, 58-59

Picture credits
t=top b=bottom l=left r=right c=centre

Angela Murphy 7bl, 23cl
Bridgeman Art Library 62lc
British Museum (Natural History) 6r, 15bl, 19 bc
Bruce Coleman 7bc?, 10l, 62tr, 63br
Mansell Collection 8 cl, 9br, 13c, 17tr, 27bc, 33tl, 36tc, 36lc, 38c, 41rc, 42tl, 43rc, 46lc
Mary Evans Picture Library 9 tr, 16tl, 20tr, 21bc, 22br, 25br, 26tl, 30lc, 31br, 32br, 35c, 41tr, 42c, 51br, 52rc, 53tl, 54c
Museum of London 24bc, 25tl, 47c, 48bl
Peter Newark's Historical Pictures 24tl, 25cl, 28tc, 34tl, 41bc, 49br, 60tl, 60br, 61br
Ronald Sheridan's Photo-Library 22tr, 38tl, 50tl, 55r, 63br

Topham Picture Library 10bl

Illustrators
John Woodcock
John James
Mark Bergin

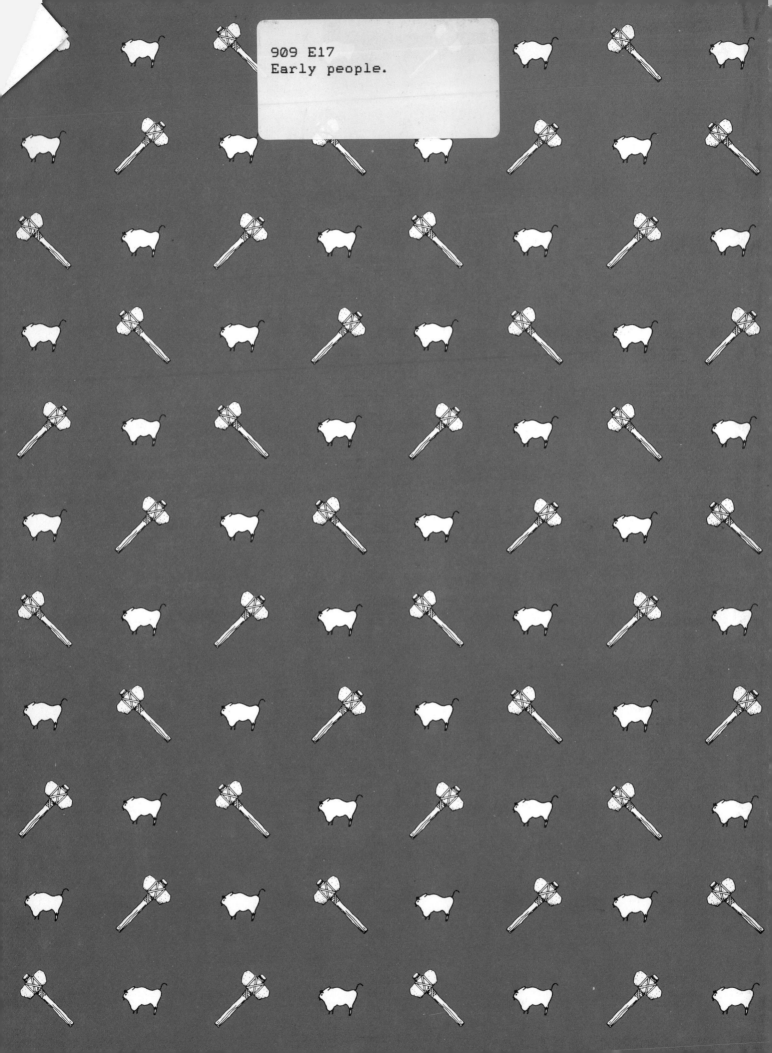